painted illusions

The Art of Cornelius Gijsbrechts

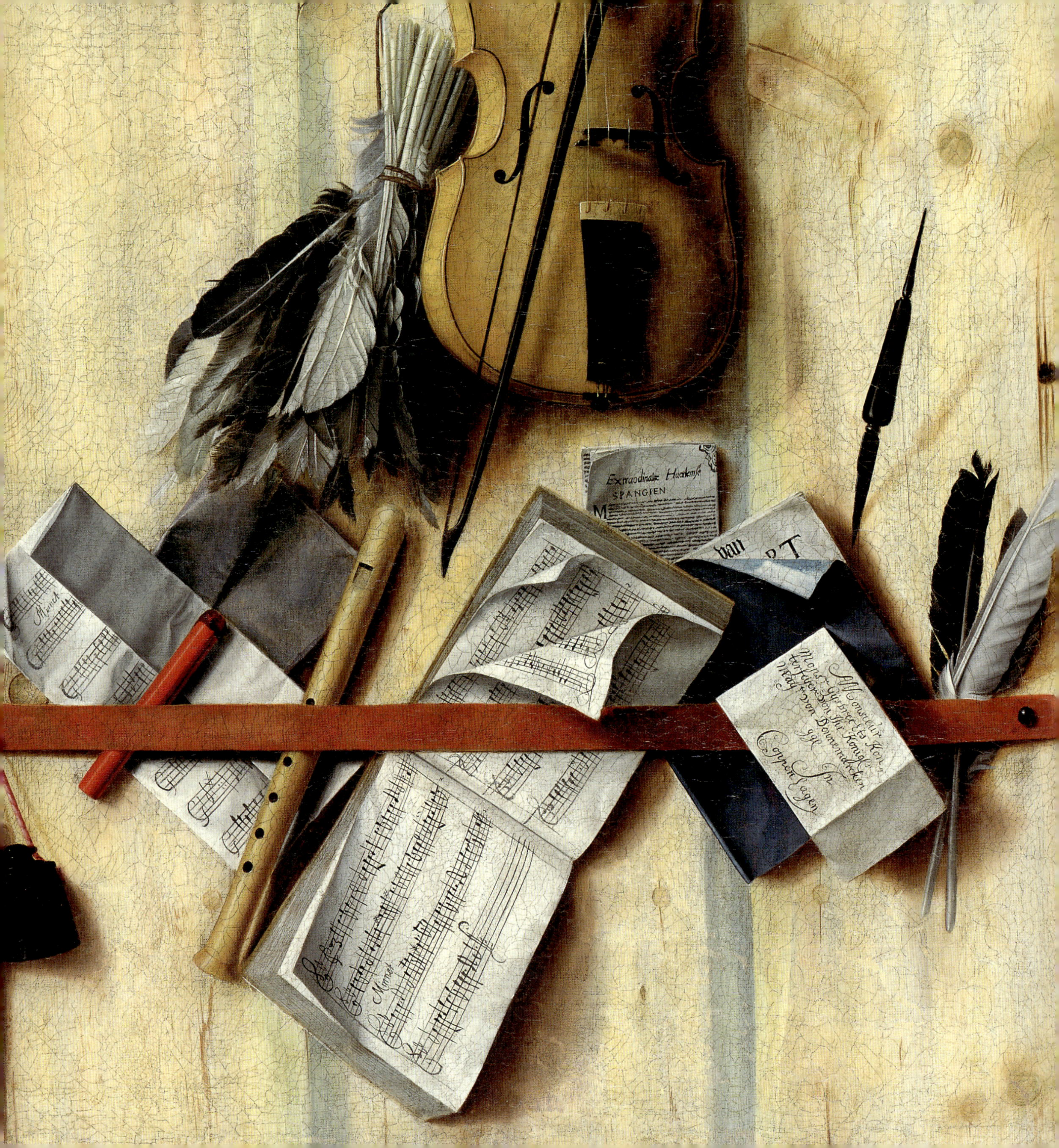

Extraodinaire Haerlemse
SPANGIEN
M
van

painted illusions

The Art of Cornelius Gijsbrechts

Olaf Koester

National Gallery Company Limited

This book was published to accompany an
exhibition at the National Gallery, London
2 February – 1 May 2000

**Supported by The Bernard Sunley
Charitable Foundation**

First published in Great Britain in 2000
by National Gallery Company Limited
St Vincent House, 30 Orange Street,
London WC2H 7HH

Reprinted 2000

ISBN 1 85709 299 6

British Cataloguing-in-Publication Data.
A catalogue record is available from the
British Library.

Editors Caroline Bugler and Mandi Gomez
Designer Chloë Alexander

Typeset in Monotype Bell
Printed and bound in Great Britain by
Butler & Tanner Ltd, Frome and London

Cover illustrations
Front: **Trompe l'Oeil of a Letter Rack with
Christian V's Proclamation** (cat. no. 3)
Back: **Trompe l'Oeil. The Reverse of a
Framed Painting** (cat. no. 23)
Frontispiece: **Trompe l'Oeil with Violin,
Music Book and Recorder** (cat. no. 8, detail)

All illustrations are of works by Cornelius
Gijsbrechts unless otherwise stated

Author's Acknowledgements

AT THE STATENS MUSEUM for Kunst, Copenhagen, I would like to acknowledge
the contributions of Henrik Bjerre, Head of Conservation, and Mette Bjarnhof,
Lone Bøgh and Pauline Lehmann who were responsible for cleaning and restoring
the Statens Museum paintings.

At the National Gallery, I would like to thank Neil MacGregor for his
enthusiastic support in bringing Gijsbrechts to London, Michael Wilson, Mary
Hersov and Jo Kent of the Exhibitions Department, Caroline Bugler for her work
in editing this catalogue and David Bomford for his collaboration throughout the
organisation of the London exhibition.

Olaf Koester

Foreword

THE ART OF DECEPTION that Cornelius Gijsbrechts perfected around 1670 at the court of Denmark is perhaps the most sustained exercise in visual trickery in the history of European painting.

Playing on the borders of seeming and being, his dazzlingly accomplished painted illusions delight us as they deceive us. But they have, of course, a deeper purpose – to force us to consider the nature of things and the power of art.

To look at one of these paintings is a bit like clearing out a house: we are confronted with the detritus of a busy existence, ephemera that have outlived their creator. Pinned to a letter rack are the remorseless, beguiling, incriminating trivia with which we fill our every day. The fact that even now we cannot tell which are real and which fanciful will, depending on our mood, either convince us that all is indeed vanity, or dispel our melancholy in a gasp of astonishment. Gijsbrechts is the undisputed master of the *vanitas*.

Yet, he remains a mysterious figure, little known outside Copenhagen where he produced his illusions for two enlightened patrons, the Danish kings Frederik III and Christian V and where the bulk of his best work still remains. Visitors to the Statens Museum of Kunst in Copenhagen have long been drawn to these astonishing images and we are delighted that the present exhibition – the first time this group of paintings has been shown outside Denmark – will allow a new public in London to see them.

For this opportunity we are indebted to the Statens Museum and its Director, Allis Helleland. This is the latest in a long series of happy collaborations between our two museums over recent years, which have seen great paintings move in both directions, to the delight of both Danish and British visitors. This exhibition has been organised in collaboration with Olaf Koester, Senior Curator of Paintings at the Statens Museum and the author of this catalogue. We are grateful to him for co-ordinating arrangements in Copenhagen and for his lucid discussion of the mysterious Gijsbrechts and his extraordinary art.

Exhibitions need patrons no less than artists. The Bernard Sunley Charitable Foundation not only provided the room in which this exhibition will be held, but have funded the exhibitions in it over many years – acts of outstanding generosity for which we are very grateful.

Neil MacGregor
Director of the National Gallery

Contents

Trompe-l'oeil Painting

THE FRENCH TERM *trompe l'oeil* (meaning 'deceive the eye') is used to describe a painting that has been made with the intention of tricking viewers into believing, even if only for a brief moment, that they are faced with a real object rather than a two-dimensional image. The term was first used in this sense in 1800 when the French painter Louis-Léopold Boilly (1761–1845) exhibited a painting at the Paris Salon which was listed in the catalogue as '*Un trompe l'oeil*'. The picture in question showed a number of the artist's drawings and sketches one on top of the other; behind a broken pane of glass, all painted illusionistically. It caused such a stir that it proved necessary to place a balustrade in front to protect it from the crowd.[1]

Trompe-l'oeil painting goes back to antiquity – the Roman writer Pliny the Elder (AD 23/4–79) tells of a competition in the second half of the fifth century BC between two famous painters from Ancient Greece, Zeuxis and Parrhasios. Zeuxis painted a bunch of grapes that were so realistic that the birds flew down to peck at them. Parrhasios painted a curtain that was so lifelike that when Zeuxis came to inspect the finished work, he asked Parrhasios to draw the curtain aside and show him the painting hidden behind it! Zeuxis then had to admit defeat: he had fooled the birds, but Parrhasios had fooled him. Pliny's story became particularly famous, but there are other similar anecdotes from both Antiquity and more modern times, for instance the story of Giotto (1266/7–1337) deceiving his master, Cimabue (*c*.1240–1302?), into trying to waft away an illusionistically painted fly. Artistic problems associated with the realistic portrayal of nature preoccupied painters for many centuries, and the ability to do so was frequently used as a measure of their virtuosity and stature. Countless details in paintings from the fourteenth and fifteenth centuries reveal the artist's wish to cross the border between the image and the space occupied by the person viewing the image, employing illusionistic effects to induce the viewer into conceiving the painted object as reality.

The first surviving trompe-l'oeil painting in the modern sense is Jacopo de' Barbari's (*c*.1460/70 – before 1516) famous still life of 1504, *Partridge, Iron Gloves and Crossbow Bolt* (*fig. 1*), all shown as though hanging on a wall, followed a good century later by a trompe-l'oeil cupboard (*fig. 2*) by the German artist, Georg Flegel (*c*.1566–1638). Both paintings were unusual for their time and should be seen as precursors of later developments.[2]

Jacopo de' Barbari
Partridge, Iron Gloves and Crossbow Bolt
1504
Oil on limewood, 52 x 42.5 cm
Munich, Alte Pinakothek

Jacopo de' Barbari's still life may be seen as the first trompe-l'oeil painting in the modern sense. It was highly unusual for its time and was the precursor of later developments in the genre.

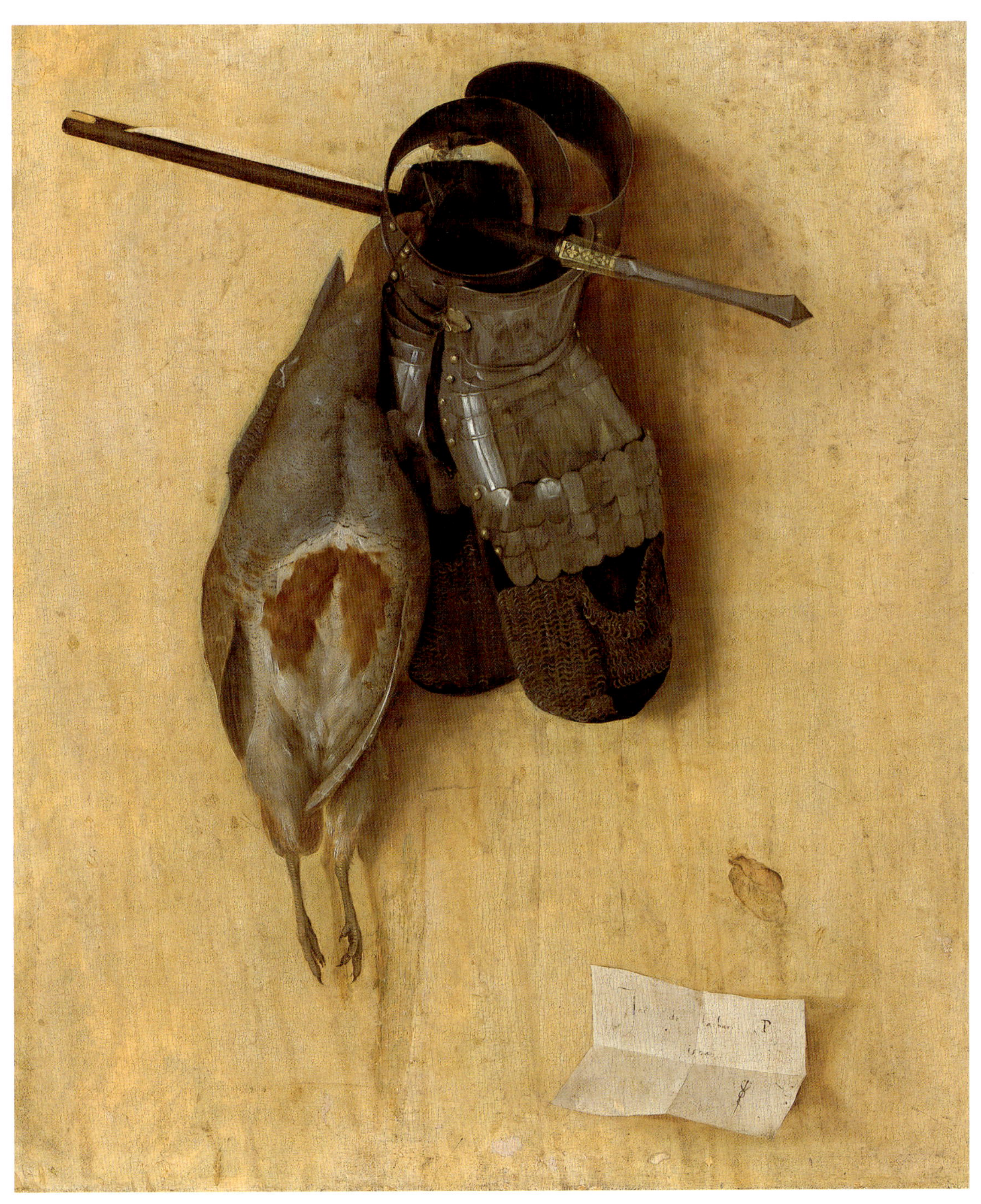

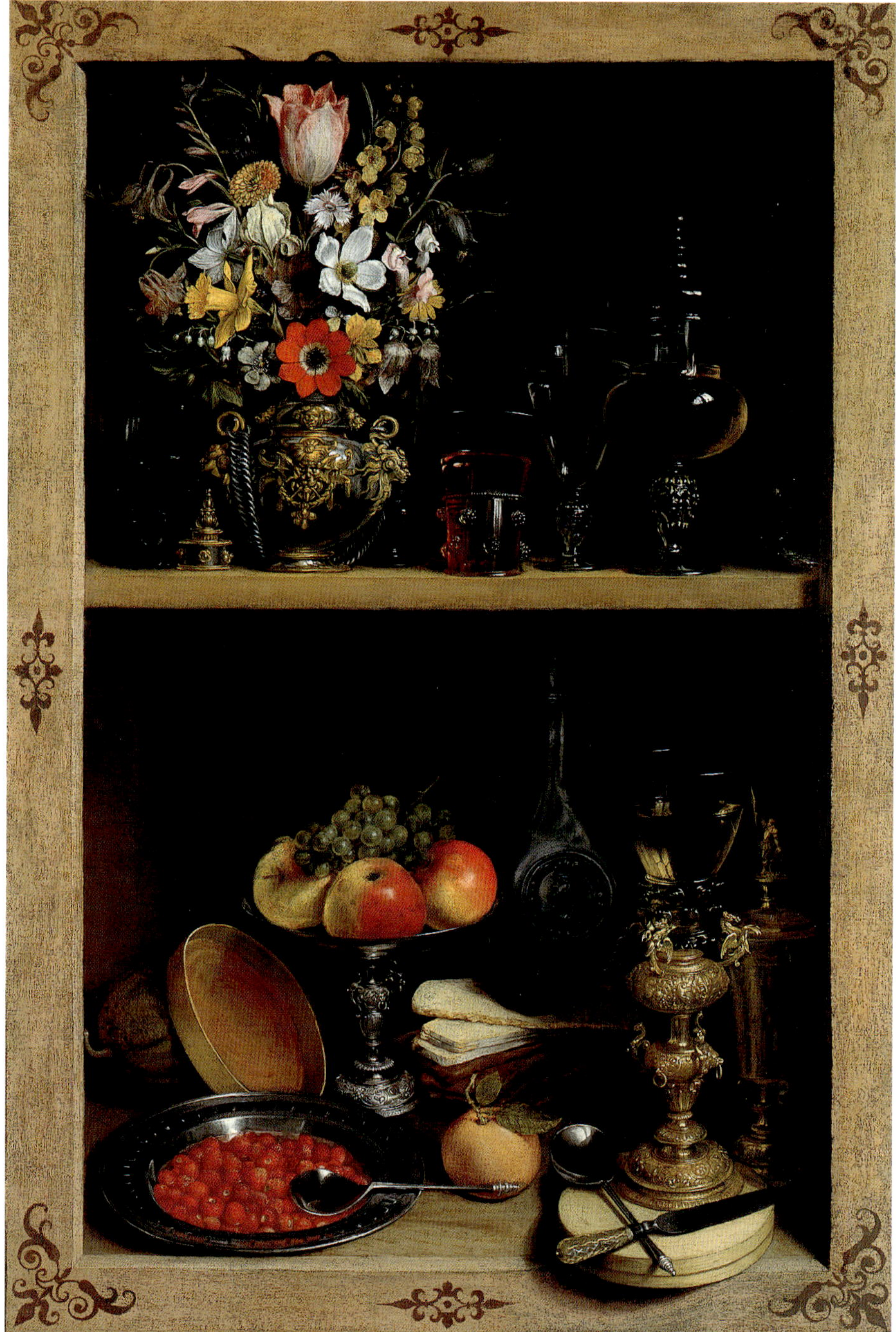

Georg Flegel
Cupboard with Bouquet of Flowers and Fruit
About 1610
Oil on canvas, 92 x 62 cm
Prague, Národni galerie v Praze

Flegel has painted a cupboard in which a number of objects are displayed. An arrangement of flowers in a metallic vase stands next to a display of glass on the top shelf. Below, various fruits are exquisitely painted together with a range of precious artefacts and domestic objects.

Trompe-l'oeil painting as a separate genre of still-life art emerged in Holland in the 1650s, when many artists – headed by two from the circle around Rembrandt: Carel Fabritius (1622–1654) and Samuel van Hoogstraten (1627–1678) – showed a particular interest in perspective and illusion. One characteristic of seventeenth-century Dutch art was the high degree of specialisation, often linked to local schools, displayed by individual artists, and the still-life genre was no exception. A number of still-life painters, especially in Delft, Amsterdam, The Hague and Dordrecht, took up the new trompe-l'oeil genre, which soon split into different types of motifs. Some artists painted dead birds suspended on a wall; others concentrated almost exclusively on hunting implements, others again on letter racks, and so on. In each case it was accepted practice to paint the various items as if protruding from a flat, neutral background, typically a board or a monochrome plaster wall. With the help of perspective, modelling, light and shade and colour and texture, the artist sought to make the objects appear palpable to the viewer, to create the illusion that these items were actually in the room and that the surface on which they rest in the picture – the board partition or wall portrayed on the canvas – constituted the limit of this room. The perspective was as shallow as possible, as the success of the illusionistic effect would otherwise depend too heavily on where the viewer was standing in relation to the picture. In seventeenth-century Holland such pictures were called *oogenbedrieger*, *schijnbedrieger* or *bedriegertje* ('eye-deceiving', 'deceptive appearance picture' or 'deceiving picture'), and, as they present at least a portion of the world as an illusion or deceit, they contain an inherent *vanitas* element (a reminder of the vanity of life). Some of the artists of the period also combined the more traditional *vanitas* still life with trompe-l'oeil painting, and on occasion the trompe-l'oeil genre became an instrument for the artist's reflections on his own profession and on the fundamental questions concerning the art of painting.

Cornelius Gijsbrechts

CORNELIUS GIJSBRECHTS did not contribute to developments in trompe-l'oeil painting in Holland during the 1650s, but it is certainly on the basis of these that his own emergence as a trompe-l'oeil artist in the 1660s and 1670s should be viewed.[3] Although – at least to a modern eye – Gijsbrechts was one of the most important artists of the seventeenth-century in the genre, information on his life and work is scarce. He is not mentioned in the art-historical literature of the time.[4] We do not know when he was born or where and when he died, neither do we know where he trained or who his teacher was – he enters the history of art seemingly from nowhere and disappears equally mysteriously. It seems probable that he was born in Antwerp – his middle name, Norbertus, suggests that he was a Catholic, and Saint Norbertus (1085–1136), the founder of the Premonstratensian Order, was himself very closely associated with Antwerp.[5]

During Gijsbrechts's stay in Denmark, he was referred to as 'the Brabant [i.e. Flemish] painter' in the royal court accounts.[6] If he is the '*Cornelis Ghijsbrecht*' who received over a hundred guilders for tasks including the repair of the city banners of Delft in 1629, and who in 1630 was among the '*Jongen*' making payments, as its masters, to the Guild of Saint Luke in The Hague,[7] he might have been born about 1610. However, on the basis of known dated works, it is more likely that our Cornelius Gijsbrechts was not born until later. In the guild year 1659–60, one '*Cornelis-Norbert Gysebrechts schilder*' (painter) became a master in the Guild of Saint Luke in Antwerp, and on 16 November 1659, also in Antwerp, '*Cornelis Norberti Gysbrechts*' became a member of the *Sodaliteit der bejaerde jongmans*,[8] a fraternity of bachelors whose members undertook to support each other in case of illness or inability to work. Members of this fraternity had at one time included Van Dyck.[9]

Cornelius Gijsbrechts seems to have travelled to Germany early in the 1660s; there are several *vanitas* still lifes by him containing proclamations and documents with German text around this time, the earliest from 1661.[10] In 1664 he was in Regensburg, for he is without doubt the painter '*Corneille*' whom the French nobleman and connoisseur Balthasar de Monconys met while staying in the town according to his travel diary, and who painted fruit pieces and '*porte lettres*' (i.e. letter racks). Gijsbrechts brought one of his fruit pieces and a trompe-l'oeil letter rack to de Monconys, having been introduced by the painter Jan van Ossenbeeck (1624–1674), who worked for the Emperor, and de Monconys bought the letter rack.[11] The status of Regensburg as seat of the German Parliament and the

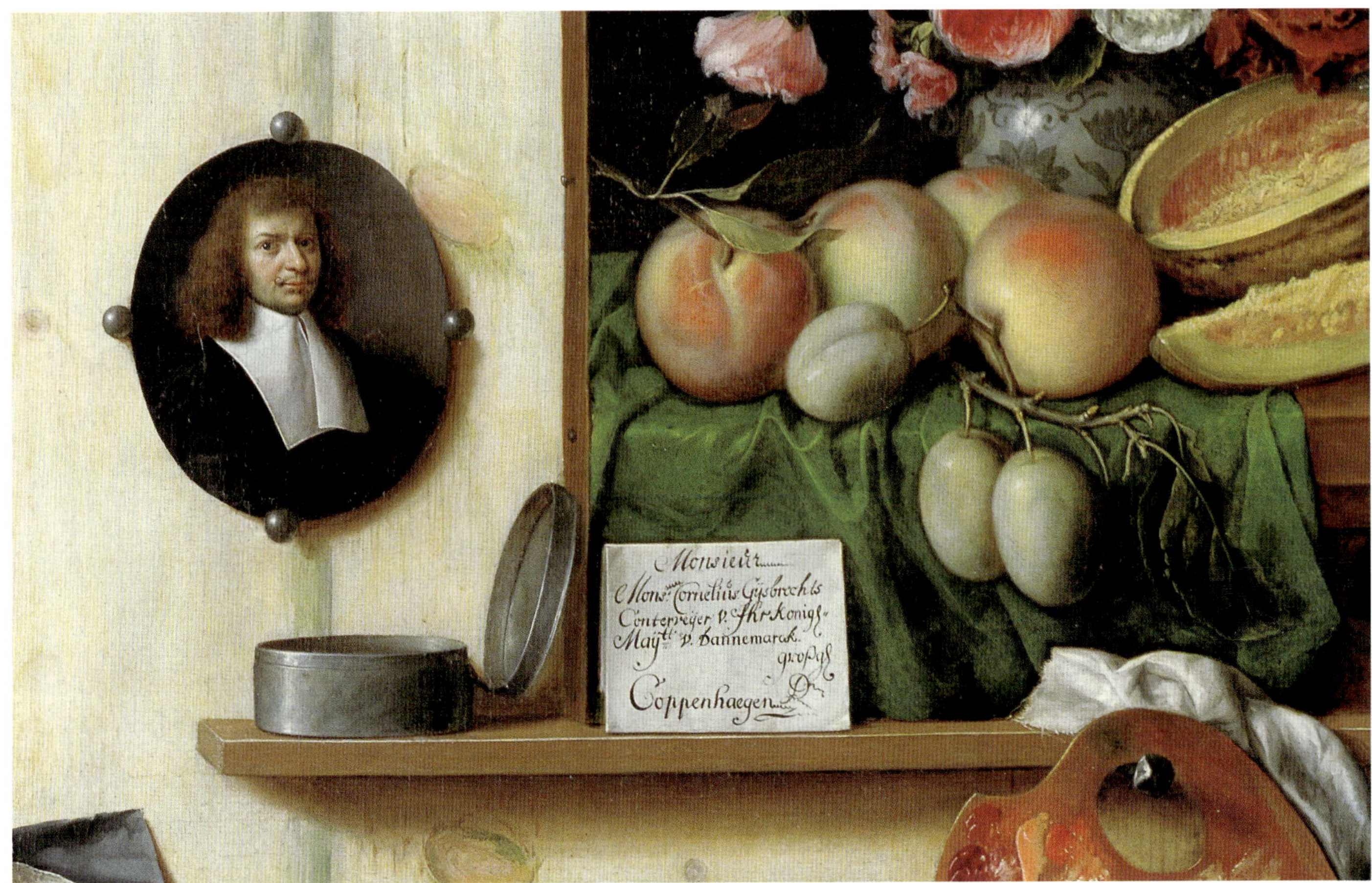

Cornelius Gijsbrechts
Detail of cat. no. 7
Trompe l'Oeil. Paintings, Painter's Tools and a Flower-Patterned Table-Cover in the Artist's Studio

Probably about 1670-72
Oil on canvas, 132 x 199 cm
Copenhagen, Statens Museum for Kunst

The painting seen in this detail is the finest of the few known small oval self portraits by Gijsbrechts. A note addressed to him can be seen in the centre.

presence of the imperial court may well have attracted Gijsbrechts there, but it is also possible that he knew of the success that Samuel van Hoogstraten had achieved with his trompe-l'oeil pictures in Regensburg and, in particular, in Vienna with Emperor Ferdinand III, some ten years earlier. However it is not known whether Gijsbrechts managed to obtain commissions from Emperor Leopold I and his court.

Between 1664–5 and 1668 Gijsbrechts was probably working in Hamburg; there is certainly a strong tradition that he was active in the city.[12] It seems likely that he met there the German still-life and trompe-l'oeil painter Georg Hinz (or Hainz; 1630/1–1668), who worked in Altona and Hamburg and had connections with the courts in Denmark and Gottorp.

Cornelius Gijsbrechts in Copenhagen

GIJSBRECHTS WORKED IN Copenhagen from 1668 to 1672 as court painter to the Danish king Frederik III (born 1609, reigned 1648–70) and his successor Christian V (born 1646, reigned 1670–99). Frederik III had summoned Gijsbrechts to Denmark in September 1668, possibly from Hamburg.[13] The King was profoundly interested in science, and in addition he was a born collector, whose interest in antiques, works of art and, above all, books, had been awakened in his youth during visits to the Netherlands and France in 1628–30. In 1650 he established the Royal *Kunstkammer* (Cabinet of Curiosities) in Copenhagen Castle, but when the available space in the castle became too restricted, he set about constructing a special building from 1665 – the present-day *Rigsarkivet* (National Archives) – for both the *Kunstkammer* and his large library. It was not completed until about 1675 under his successor, Christian V, and by the end of the 1670s the collections had finally been transferred to their new home. In addition to paintings and sculptures, the *Kunstkammer* contained natural specimens, artefacts, ethnographical specimens, coins and all manner of curiosities. Frederik III's interest in rarities and the art of the time spread over a wide field – from such celebrated artists as Jacob Jordaens (1593–1678) and Salvator Rosa (1615–1673), from both of whom he bought paintings direct, to the Dutch *fijnschilder* ('fine painter'), Toussaint Gelton (active *c*.1650–80), whom he employed in Copenhagen.

In Copenhagen, Gijsbrechts was installed close to the King, being allocated a studio in the Kongens Have Park near Rosenborg Palace.[14] In Northern Europe, it appears to have been traditional for monarchs to gather a colony of their best artists and artisans around their summer residences.[15] The first tangible evidence of Gijsbrechts's presence in Copenhagen is the large *Studio Wall and Vanitas Still Life* (cat. no. 10) and two vertical letter racks (cat. nos. 1 and 2), all from 1668. These pictures may be the first he painted in Copenhagen, and one of the letter racks (cat. no. 1) is the earliest work by Gijsbrechts to incorporate a reference to the Danish king, who is portrayed in profile on a large red seal hanging from the tidy on the left. The *Studio Wall* has, however, an inscription (on a slip of paper behind the bottom-left of the still life's stretcher) in which the painter designates himself '*Conterfeyer zu Copenhagen*' (Painter in Copenhagen), but not painter to the King; this latter title only appears in pictures from 1670 on, which might indicate it was not until that year he was officially appointed court artist.

Gijsbrechts's *Studio Wall* appears not to have been followed by any similar

1 Trompe l'Oeil. Board Partition with Letter Rack and Music Book

1668
Oil on canvas, 123.5 x 107 cm
Copenhagen, Statens Museum for Kunst

A dark green curtain is pulled back and up over a curtain rod to reveal an intriguing display of letters, documents and other printed ephemera pushed behind a fixing of horizontal and vertical red tape. The light enters from the left, where, in the bottom compartment of the Bordeaux tidy, is a large red seal (detail, *below*) with a portrait of King Frederik III of Denmark in profile and the inscription FREDERICUS III DI DANNORV GOT REX along the edge. This is the artist's earliest reference to the Danish King.

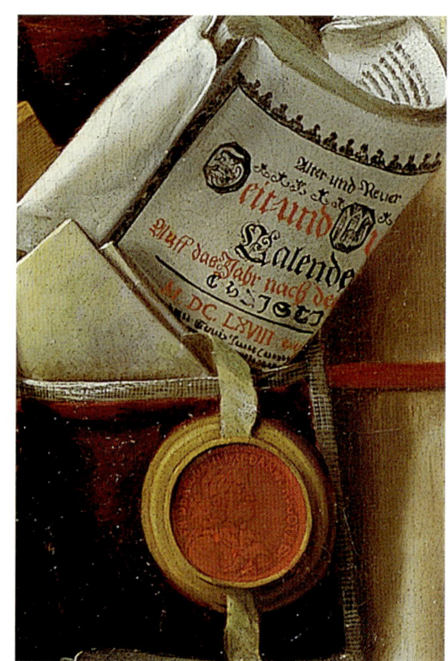

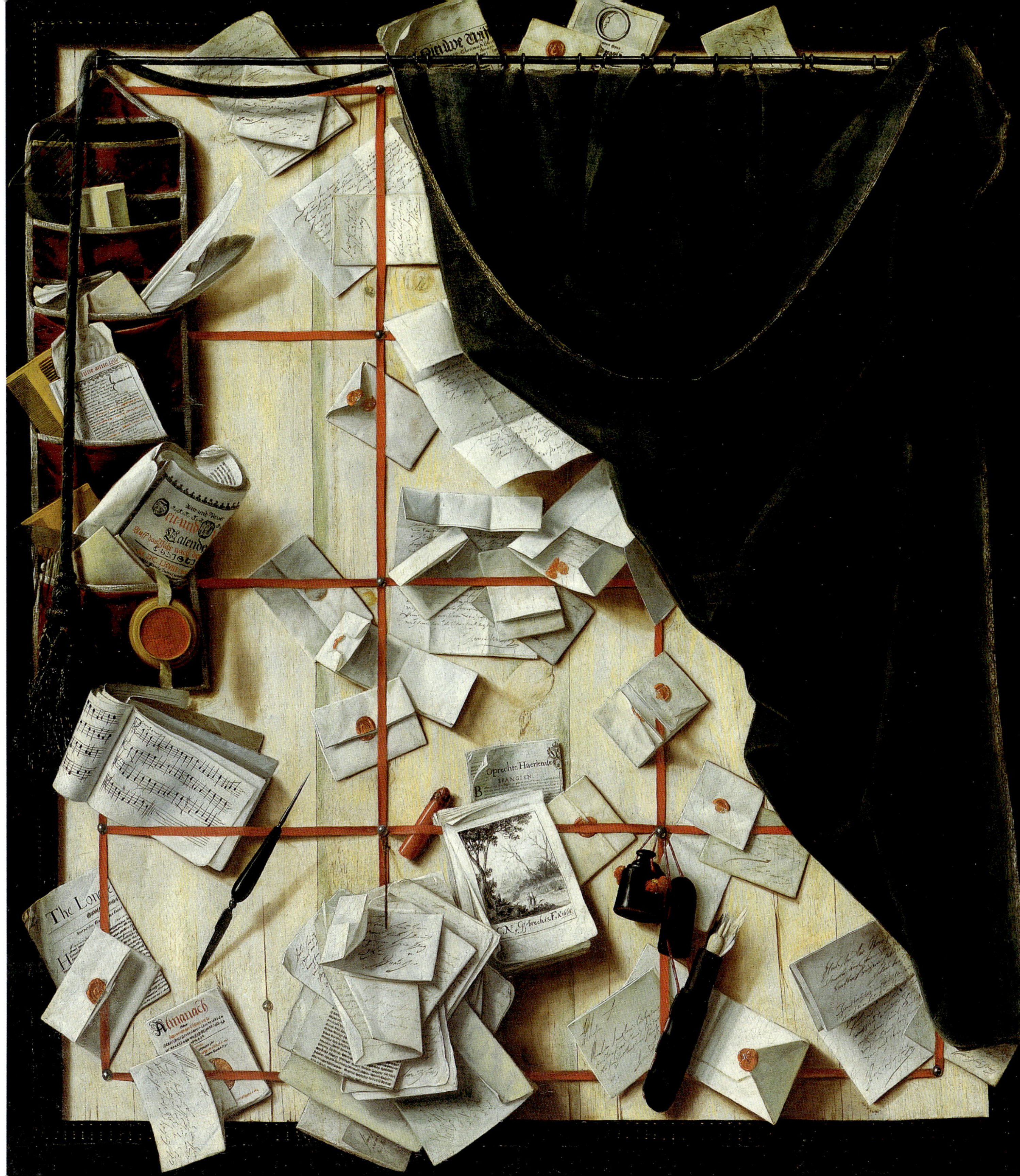

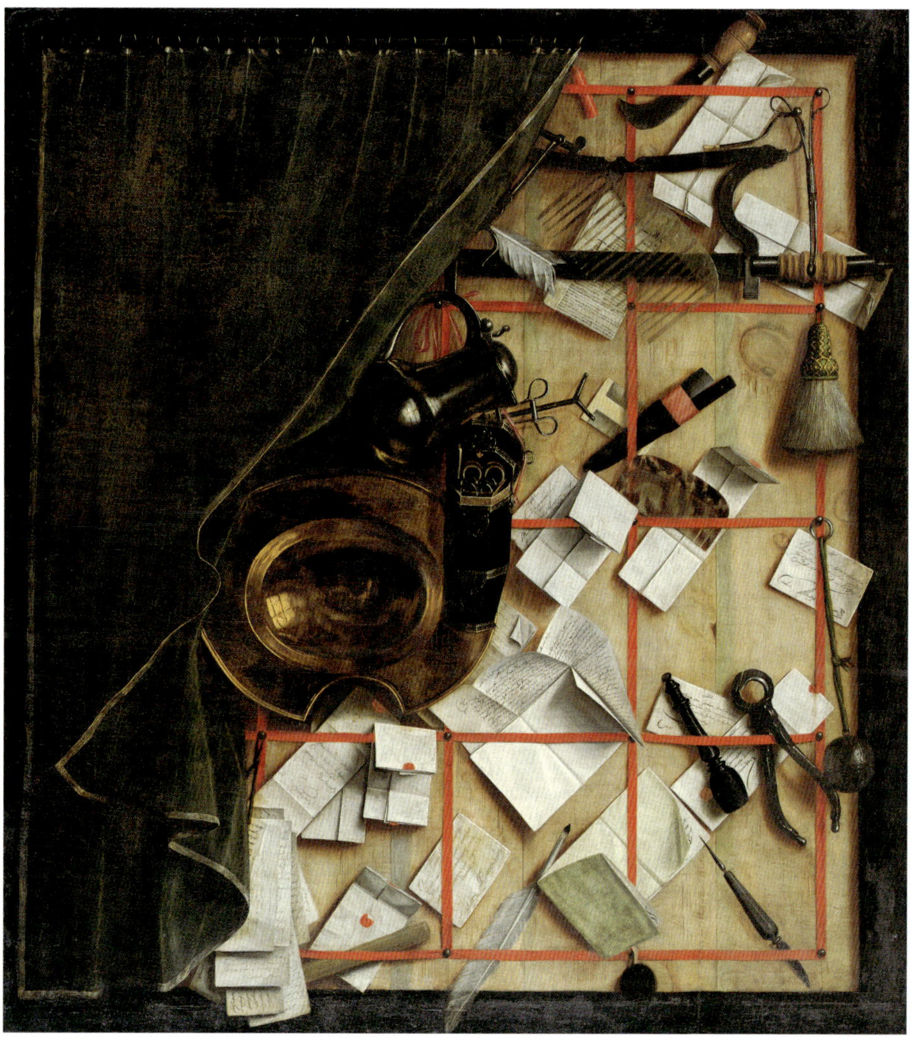

2 Trompe l'Oeil. Letter Rack with a Barber-Surgeon's Instruments

Probably about 1668
Oil on canvas, 125 x 109.5 cm
Copenhagen, Statens Museum for Kunst

A dark green curtain is pulled to the left to reveal a letter rack with a similar repertoire of objects as its companion piece (cat. no. 1). Light enters from the right to catch the artist's studio window reflected in the shaving bowl and a jug and case containing a pair of scissors and other instruments at the centre of the composition. Both pieces contain *vanitas* symbolism, although here an entire set of barber-surgeon's instruments may suggest the metaphor of purification, endorsed by the emblematic literature popular at the time.

paintings in Copenhagen, but his letter racks certainly were. Two large oblong letter racks, dating from 1671 and 1672 respectively, represent the culmination of Gijsbrechts's work in this genre (cat. nos. 3 and 4). They contain portraits and documents referring to Frederik III and Christian V, and thus reflect the change of monarch at the beginning of 1670. As none of Gijsbrechts's Danish pictures bears a date later than 1672, and as the last payment to him in the accounts for paintings executed for the King (see p. 31) is on 1 April 1672, he presumably left the country that year to go to Stockholm.

Gijsbrechts remained in Stockholm for perhaps a couple of years – on 4 April 1674 he acknowledged payment for a painting he had sold to the Swedish Chancellor, Count Magnus Gabriel De la Gardie (1622–1686).[16] He must then have returned to Germany, for in 1675 he was probably in Breslau (present-day Wroclaw in Poland) – a letter addressed to '*Monsieur Cornelius Gijsbrechts*' in Breslau can be seen among the many letters in a painting from 1675 now in Warsaw. This is Gijsbrechts's last dated work, and after 1675 his fate is unknown.

Gijsbrechts's Work and the Danish Royal Collections

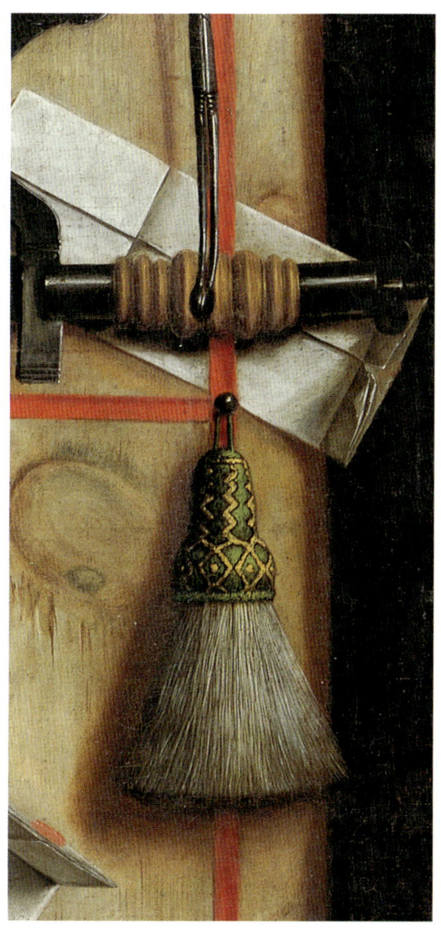

THE NEW *KUNSTKAMMER* building, started under Frederik III, was completed by his son, Christian V, in 1675. The collections were moved from Copenhagen Castle to the top floor of the new building, an operation completed around 1680. Gijsbrechts's activities in Copenhagen thus coincided to some extent with the initial expansion of the *Kunstkammer* and with the erection from about 1665 of the new building for both library and *Kunstkammer*. As Gijsbrechts's works of the time contain reproductions of works of art and other items from the royal collections, and the trompe-l'oeil genre seems an ideal form of art for a *Kunstkammer*, there has been a tendency to assume that Gijsbrechts's works were almost exclusively intended for the *Kunstkammer*.

Existing documents do not immediately support this assumption: there is only one picture by Gijsbrechts – the large *Easel* (cat. no. 22) – in the *Kunstkammer* inventory for 1673/4, one or two years after the artist had left the country.[17] By the inventory of 1690, ten years after the move to the new building had been completed, there is mention of twelve unspecified works along with the *Easel*,[18] and only in the inventory from 1737 is there a reference to eighteen unspecified works plus the *Easel*,[19] a number broadly corresponding to those known today.[20] It should be pointed out that Christian V's private accounts show that Gijsbrechts executed at least nine paintings for Rosenborg Palace;[21] and that three of the surviving works which today are in Frederiksborg and Rosenborg were never in the *Kunstkammer*, but went straight to Rosenborg. Significantly, most of Gijsbrechts's Danish works were painted either as companion pieces or as a series, and this might suggest that they were not painted for the *Kunstkammer* but formed part of specific decorative schemes in the embellishment of rooms for the Palace.

The Art of Cornelius Gijsbrechts

ORNELIUS GIJSBRECHTS'S surviving oeuvre consists of some seventy works. Of these a very large number – about forty – are signed and dated, although on some the artist's name is found solely as part of an address on a letter, note or the like, and not as a signature in the strict sense. Various works, however, do bear his name both as an addressee in the picture's own context and in the form of a true signature carefully placed to take into account the picture's trompe-l'oeil character. About ten further works are signed but not dated.[22]

Vanitas Still Lifes

The earliest works we know by Cornelius Gijsbrechts are traditional *vanitas* still lifes, some very large, in both horizontal and vertical formats.[23] The first dated example is from 1657,[24] and surviving works suggest that until about 1662 Gijsbrechts concentrated mainly on painting such images. They generally have similar compositions: on a table covered by an oriental carpet, a number of traditional objects symbolising death and the transience of human life are gathered together. In the middle is a skull wreathed by ears of corn, a vase of flowers and an official proclamation in the form of a hand-written document hanging over the edge of the table (*fig. 3*). Many of the objects in these early *vanitas* still lifes later make regular appearances in Gijsbrechts's trompe-l'oeil works.

After 1662 only a small number of pure *vanitas* still lifes by Gijsbrechts are known.[25] They are highly simplified in comparison to the earlier works, with only a small number of objects, usually placed in an illusionistically painted niche surmounted by a rounded arch.[26] It is *vanitas* still lifes of this type which, along with fruit pieces, often constitute the 'picture within a picture' in Gijsbrechts's trompe-l'oeil depictions of studio walls (for instance cat. no. 10).

From about 1662–3, Gijsbrechts specialised in trompe-l'oeil still lifes, ranging over all the established genres: letter racks (also known as '*porte-lettres*'), musical instruments hanging from boards, trompe-l'oeil cupboards, boards with hunting implements or hunting trophies attached, studio walls with depictions of trompe-l'oeil paintings, and finally the so-called *chantournés* – trompe-l'oeil pictures cut out in wood or canvas.

Cornelius Gijsbrechts
Vanitas Still Life with Skull and Bunch of Flowers
1661
Oil on canvas, 82 x 65.5 cm
Wasserburg-Anholt, Bildersammlung der Fürst zu Salm-Salm

This painting is one of Gijsbrechts's earliest *vanitas* still lifes. On the table is a collection of various symbols of the transience of human life, common to the genre. A skull surrounded by a wreath of corn suggests the inevitability of death; a pocket watch and handwritten proclamation (detail *below*) remind the viewer of the ineluctability of time and that even power is subject to transience. The proclamation refers to Philip IV of Spain (reigned 1621–65), but it is not clear what the letters inscribed at the bottom of the document mean in this context.

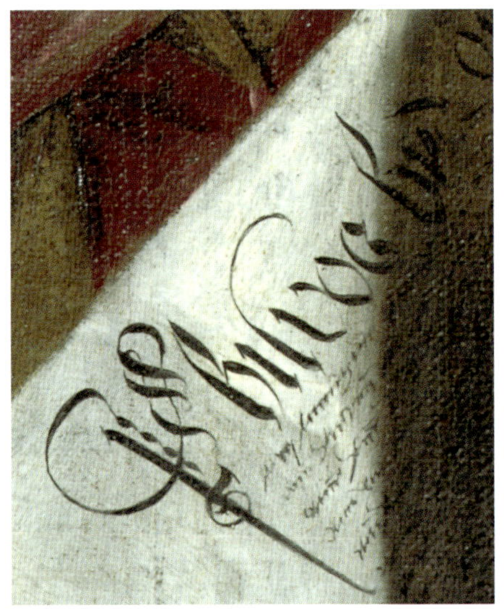

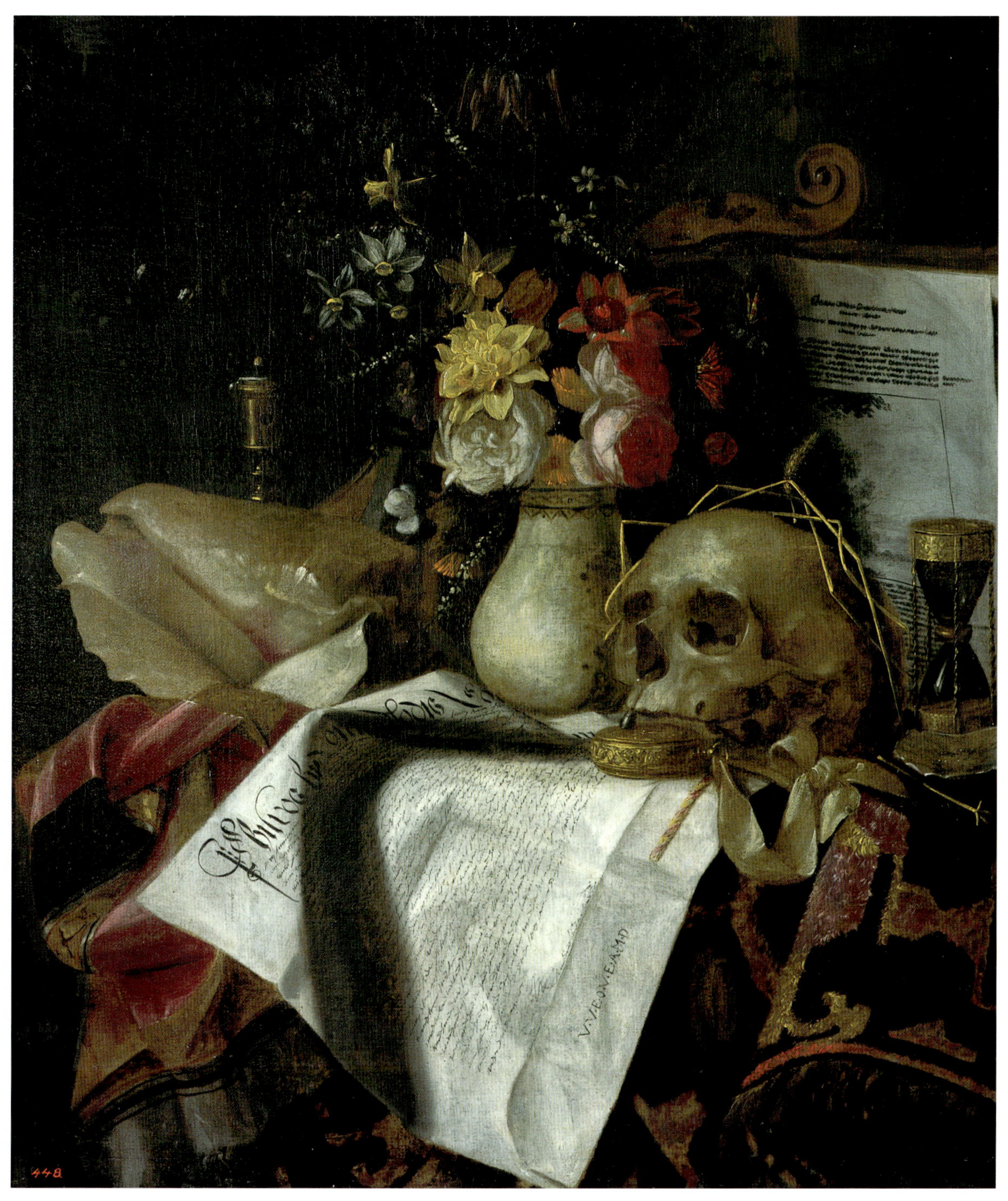

Letter Racks

GIJSBRECHTS'S EARLIEST KNOWN trompe-l'oeil still life, dated 1662, represents a board to which a few objects are attached[27] – at the top are a small painting and a print with crumpled edges, at the bottom a letter, a playing card, a comb and a recorder pushed behind a red ribbon. It is not until 1664 in a pair of paintings now in Ghent (*figs. 5 and 6*) that we see Gijsbrechts's famous letter racks constructed in their typical manner. In both, red tapes are fixed horizontally, vertically and diagonally across a yellowish-brown board. Behind them letters and documents have been placed, together with an almanac, a stick of sealing wax and other writing implements. On the first of them (*fig. 5*), there is also a picture frame with broken glass, a post horn, a pistol and a kit (small violin) with a bow, while the other (*fig. 6*) includes an hour-glass, a pair of scissors and shaving implements. They both have a green curtain on a rod fixed to the top of the board; in the first the curtain has been drawn aside towards the left and turned up over the rod, on the companion piece the curtain is drawn to the right. An illusionistic black frame surrounds each picture.

This idea of placing illusionistically painted pieces of paper in a picture goes back to the fifteenth century, when some artists began to include so-called *cartellini* in their paintings – realistic depictions of slips of paper, typically furnished with the artist's signature and the date. The oldest surviving painting of a letter rack is by the Venetian painter Vittore Carpaccio (*c.*1460/5–1525/6), on the reverse of his *Hunt on the Lagoon*, which can be dated to the 1490s (*fig. 4*).[28] Several letters and documents have been pushed down behind a tape, fixed horizontally across a window frame. The resemblance to seventeenth-century paintings of letter racks, including those by Gijsbrechts, is striking.

Gijsbrechts, however, found the immediate inspiration for his letter racks in contemporary Dutch art, and in particular from artists such as Samuel van Hoogstraten, who worked mainly in his native Dordrecht but also on occasion in Vienna and London (*fig. 7*). Throughout the 1660s and the early 1670s, Gijsbrechts created letter racks with ever larger and more complex compositions. Two companion pieces in Copenhagen, one with the green curtain drawn back to the left (cat. no. 2) and the other with the curtain drawn back and turned up on the curtain rail on the right (cat. no. 1), are fundamentally of the same type as the Ghent pictures of four years earlier, but they are larger and have a more settled composition. The Ghent pictures' mixture of horizontal, vertical and diagonal

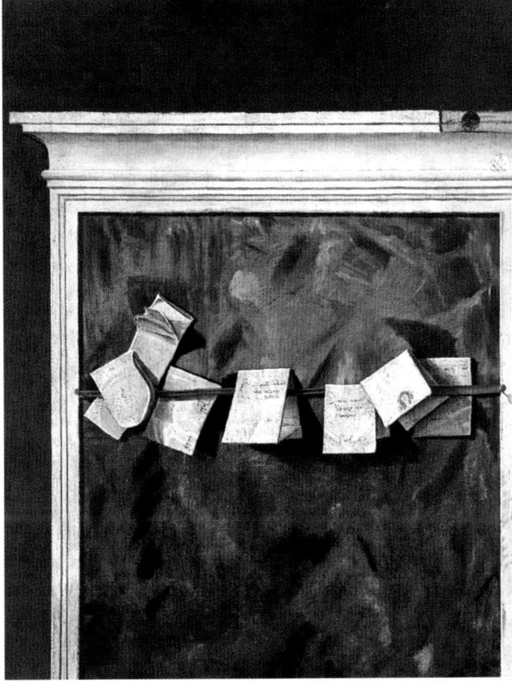

Fig. 4

Vittore Carpaccio
Letter Rack
1490s
Oil on wood, 75.4 x 63.8 cm
Los Angeles, The J. Paul Getty Museum

This letter rack is on the reverse of Carpaccio's *Hunt on the Lagoon*. The resemblance to Gijsbrechts's letter racks is striking. In the fifteenth century several artists included so-called *cartellini*, or small pieces of paper in their paintings, but Carpaccio goes somewhat further than this to show a tape with several pieces of printed matter tucked behind it.

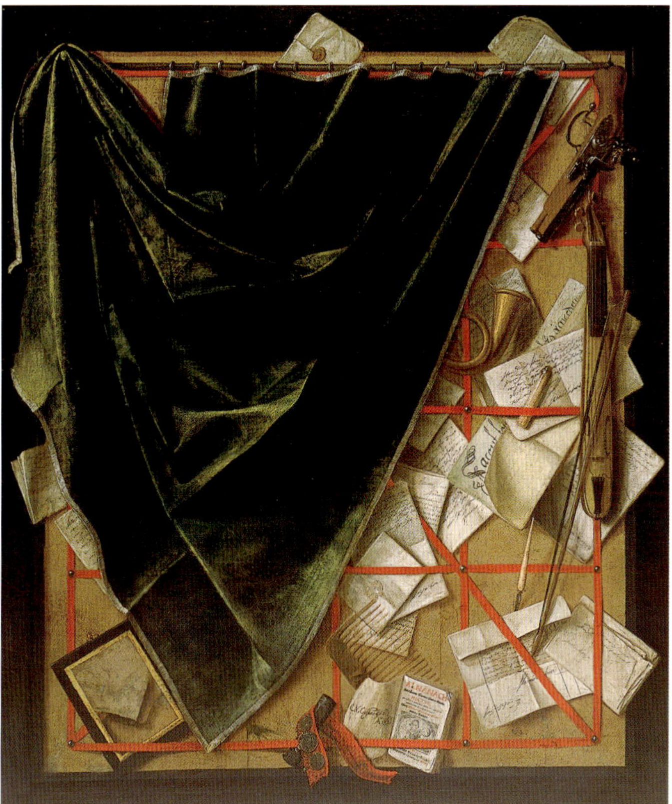

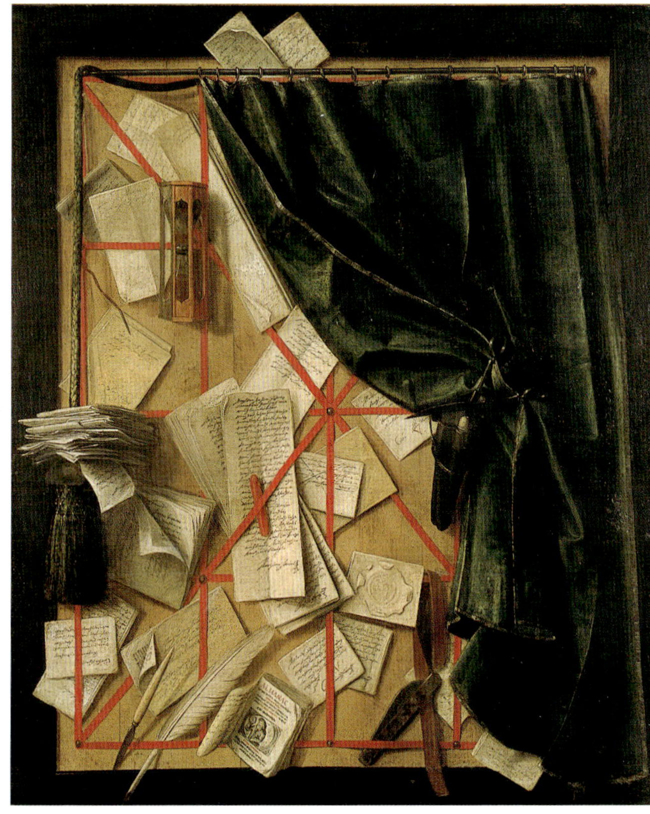

ribbons has been replaced by a tight chessboard pattern of horizontal and vertical ribbons and a larger number and greater variety of objects join the letters and documents. One of the pictures (cat. no. 2) includes a barber's shaving bowl and a whole set of a barber-surgeon's instruments, while in the other a tidy is suspended on the wall, containing several compartments filled with combs, quill pens, letters, a calendar and so on. The tidy, a device also used by van Hoogstraten,[29] appears frequently in Gijsbrechts's letter racks, for instance also in two horizontal paintings in Copenhagen, dated respectively 1671 (cat. no. 3) and 1672 (cat. no. 4).

These two letter racks are the culmination of Gijsbrechts's work in this genre. They contain an enormously rich variety of objects and, as discussed on page 25, also include direct references to the two Danish kings on the throne in the course of Gijsbrechts's stay in Copenhagen. At the centre of the 1671 picture (cat. no. 3) there is a large proclamation from Christian V; in the bottom left-hand corner there is a print of a portrait of Christian V dressed in the garb of a Roman emperor,

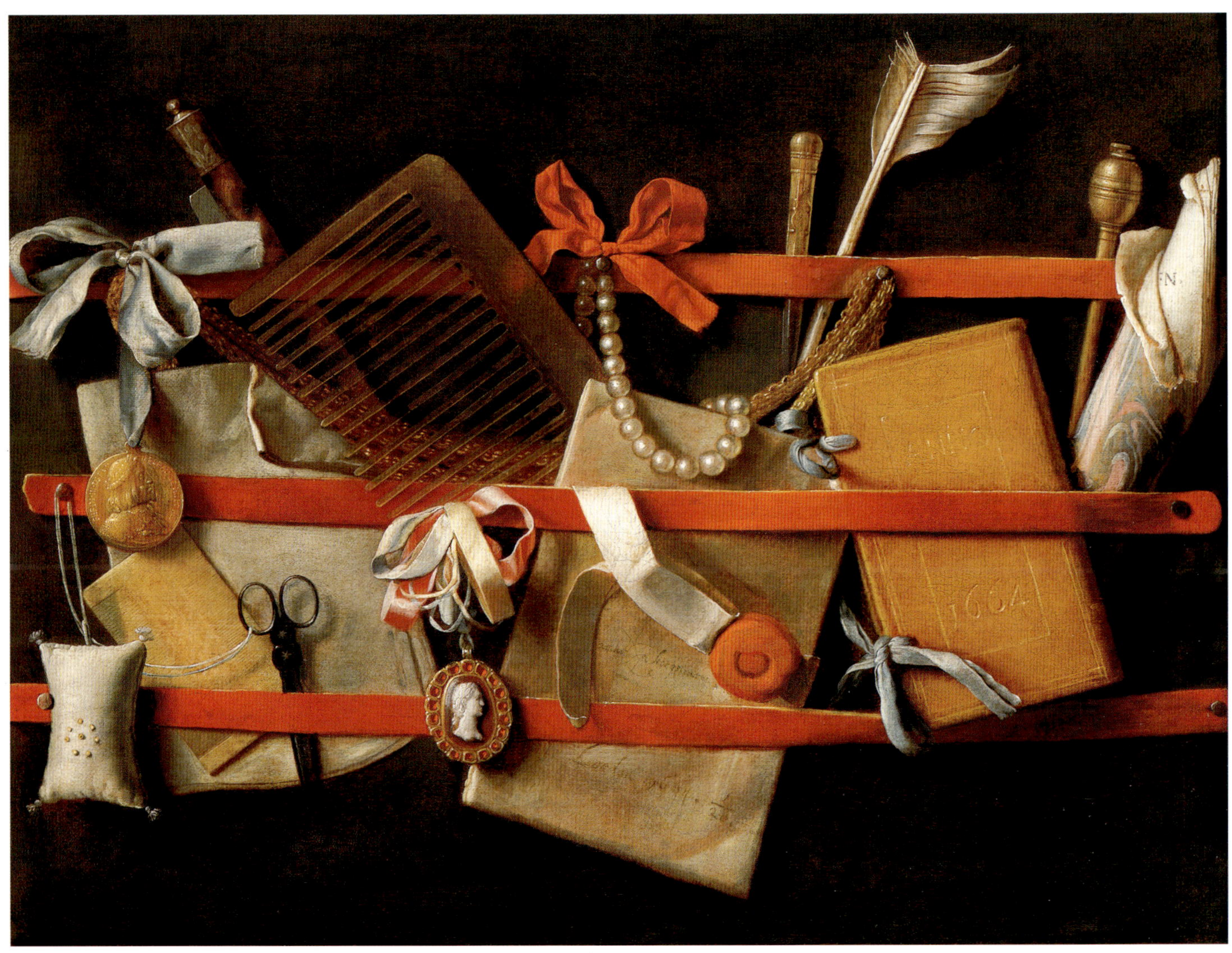

above which is a small oval portrait of the late Frederik III. The 1672 picture (cat. no. 4) is rather more restrained in its royal references, containing only a proclamation by Frederik III at its centre.

A small number of works from the 1670s represent a new type of picture in Gijsbrechts's oeuvre. They depict objects gathered against a wall, but dispense with the curtain, the painted frame and the grid of tapes where a combination of objects are composed in a seemingly random way, as in cat. no. 8 on page 31.

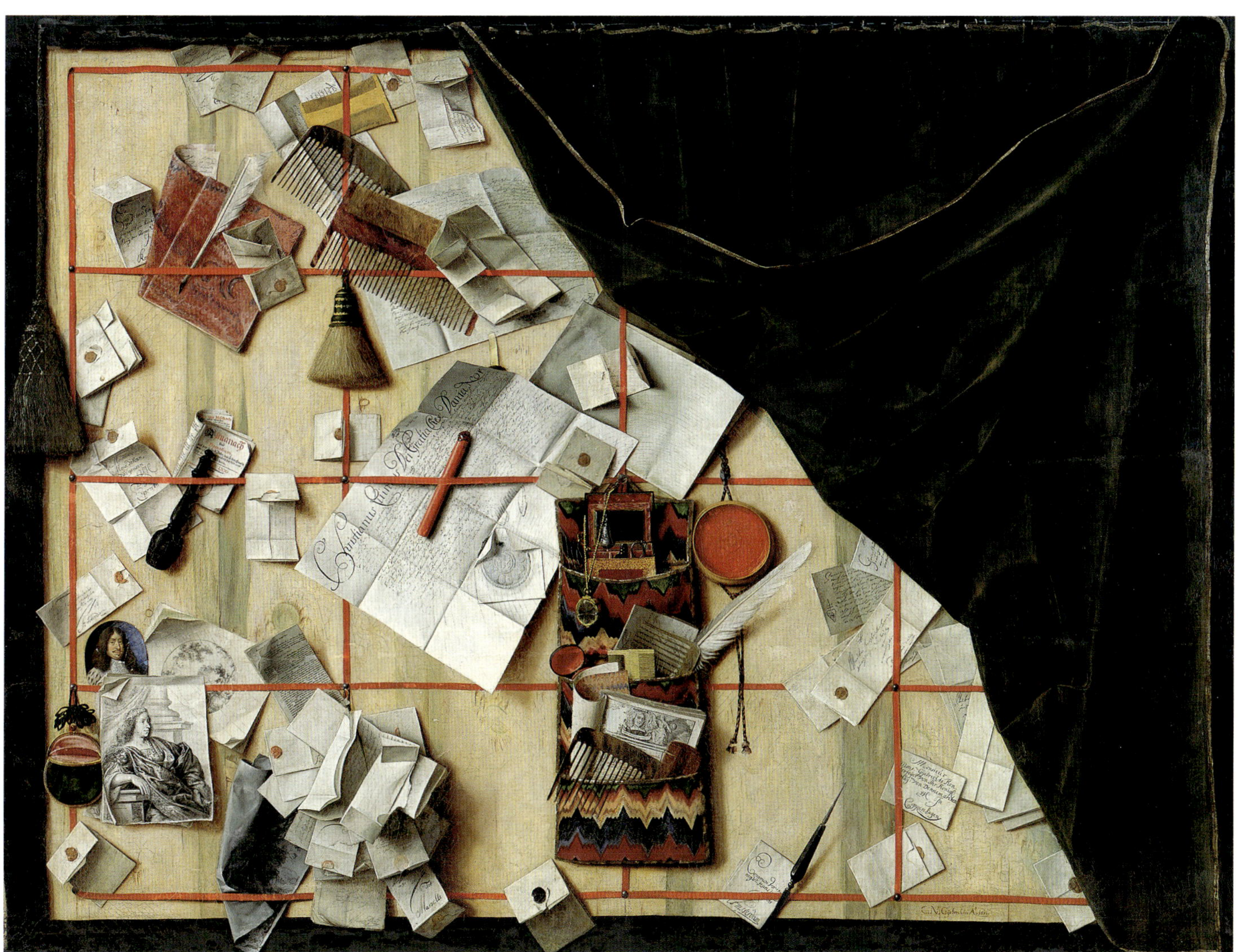

3 Trompe l'Oeil of a Letter Rack with Christian V's Proclamation

1671
Oil on canvas, 138.5 x 183 (181.5) cm
Copenhagen, Statens Museum for Kunst

A curtain is pulled back to the right to reveal a regular chessboard pattern of red tape. A collection of letters, printed ephemera, writing implements and so on have been pushed behind the tapes while at the centre of the composition is a proclamation from King Christian V of Denmark celebrating his sovereignty over Denmark and Norway. An engraving in the bottom left-hand corner shows a portrait of Christian V as a Roman emperor, and just above this is a small oval portrait of Frederick III after Karel van Mander. To the right, is a marbled tidy containing a pocket watch, toilette set, scissors and other implements of this sort, probably symbolic of spiritual cleansing. Such metaphors were popular in contemporary emblematic literature.

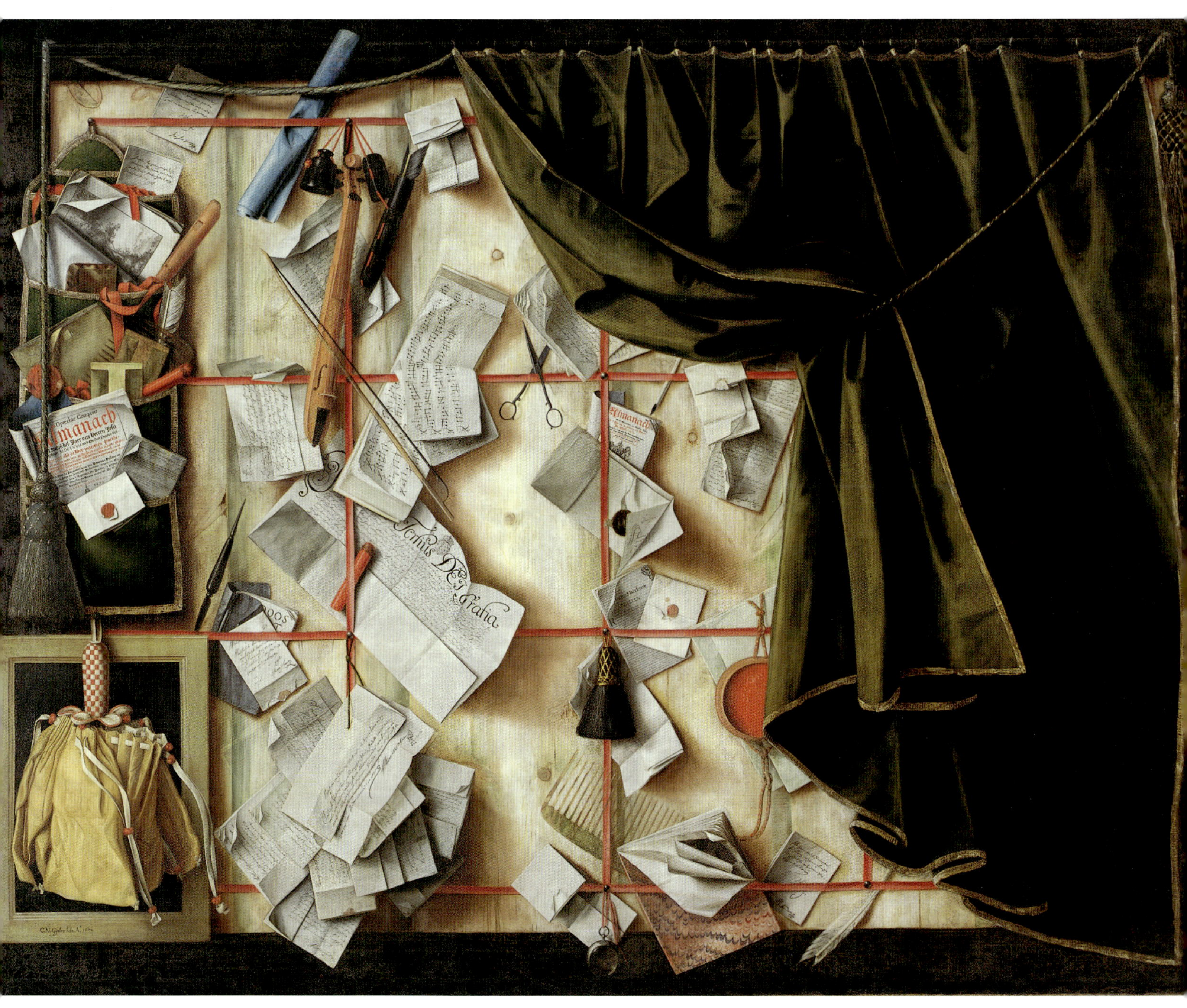

The Meaning of *Quodlibet* Paintings

4 Trompe l'Oeil of a Letter Rack with Proclamation by Frederik III

1672
Oil on canvas, 145.5 x 183 cm
Copenhagen, Statens Museum for Kunst

The picture is a companion piece to cat. no. 3, but is more restrained in its royal references. The large hand-written document at the centre of the composition is a proclamation by King Frederik III seen in the inscription below the Danish national coat of arms: Tertius Dei Gratia [(Frederik) the Third by the Grace of God . . .]. The two paintings both contain *vanitas* symbolism. For example, the watch, newspaper and almanac symbolise the ephemeral nature of time; the scissors the thread of life being cut; the musical instrument and the moneybag the transitoriness of the senses and worldly wealth, while, according to emblematic literature of the time, the brush, comb and razor symbolise spiritual cleansing.

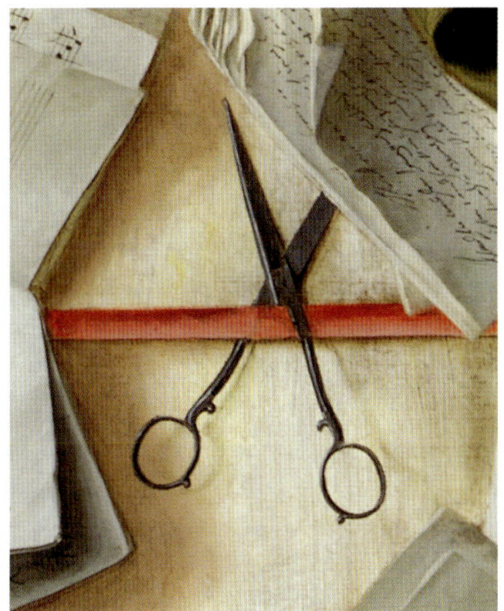

LETTER RACKS CHARACTERISTICALLY contain all kinds of apparently random objects of the kind one might have at hand for everyday use, thus a picture of this kind is often called a *'quodlibet'*, Latin for 'what you please', i.e. 'anything at all', or 'all sorts'. The fundamental elements are letters – sealed, half opened or completely unfolded – envelopes, documents, notes, writing implements such as quill pens (and their holders), penknives, sealing wax, signet stamps and ink bottles. Combs also make frequent appearances, whether as light, transparent combs, tortoiseshell combs or fine-tooth combs, along with almanacs, proclamations, pamphlets, scraps of newspapers, pocket-watches, hour-glasses, knives, scissors, prints, purses, frames containing broken glass, pistols, hunting horns, music books and musical instruments such as kits and recorders. Some of the objects we can recognise from *vanitas* iconography, and there is much to suggest that these *quodlibet* paintings, under their mundane surface, are making use of a symbolic language taken from popular emblem books, encouraging a blameless way of life, warning of the emptiness of pleasure and reminding of the ephemeral nature of earthly life. In his emblem book *Sinnepoppen* (Amsterdam 1614), Roemer Visscher included a reproduction of a comb under the title of '*Purgat et Ornat*' (It cleans and adorns), and in his popular '*Spiegel van den ouden en nieuwen tij*' ('Mirror of the Old and New Times'; Amsterdam 1658), Jacob Cats drew a parallel between combing his hair and purging his body and soul: 'Comb your hair, comb your hair, again and again, and not only your hair, but also what is hidden beneath it, right down to the bone.'[30] The pocket-watch might refer to temperance; musical instruments, especially the kit (in its use as a dancing master's violin), and music books might symbolise the emptiness of earthly pleasures; the purse and proclamations by the king and the authorities might denote the transience of riches and temporal power; the almanac the implacable march of time; the hour-glass time running out and, like the scissors (the attribute of the Fates), cutting the allotted thread of life.[31] The metaphor is more or less universal, and is rarely individualised in relation to the person commissioning or receiving the painting.

A striking feature common to the majority of the *quodlibet* pictures by Gijsbrechts is the blue-green curtain pulled aside to reveal the letter rack and its contents. All the pictures are surrounded by an illusionistically painted black frame, which throws shadows on the board. The trompe-l'oeil curtain hangs from a rod which is fixed to the top of this frame and extends right across it.[32] We know from seventeenth-century Dutch interior and genre pictures that paintings on walls were protected by providing them with a curtain. Thus the picture is not merely a trompe-l'oeil depiction of objects on a board, but is also a trompe-l'oeil picture, with a curtain that can seemingly be drawn or drawn back, of a trompe-l'oeil painting of objects on a board. This might appear to be a negation or a neutralisation of the fundamental trompe-l'oeil effect, but as an artistic idea the illusionistically painted curtain can be traced right back to Parrhasios' curtain in Pliny's anecdote about Zeuxis and Parrhasios – this anecdote was retold in seventeenth-century Holland by both Karel van Mander in *Het Schilder-boeck* (Haarlem 1604) and Philips Angel in his *Lof der Schilder-konst* (Leiden 1642),[33] and was particularly popular with artists from about the middle of the century. Gijsbrechts also employed this curtain device in other more traditional still lifes of the time, such as his *Trompe l'Oeil with Breakfast Piece and Goblets* (cat. no. 5).

Trompe-l'oeil *Kunstkammer* Paintings

TWO TROMPE-L'OEIL WORKS by Gijsbrechts from 1670 occupy something of a special position in his oeuvre thanks to their motif, shape and considerable size – the *Trompe l'Oeil with Trumpet, Celestial Globe and Proclamation by Frederick III* (cat. no. 6) and the *Trompe l'Oeil. Paintings, Painter's Tools and a Flower-Patterned Table-Cover in the Artist's Studio* (cat. no 7).[34] The two pictures probably belong together as companion pieces. They are the same size, and in both paintings objects are gathered together in an identical, illusionistically painted rectangular wooden niche or shallow box, the front edge of which corresponds to the picture surface. In addition, the light falls onto each of the two pictures from different sides (from the left in the studio picture and from the right in the picture containing the celestial globe and the trumpet). As the trompe-l'oeil effect is reinforced if the natural source of light in a room comes from the same direction as the light in the picture, the studio picture ought to have the light coming from the left, and the other from the right. So, if hung on either side of a window, the studio picture ought to hang on the right, the other on the left; if the two are hung side by side between two windows, the studio picture ought to hang on the left.

The imagery contained in both paintings strengthens their status as companion pieces. The picture with Frederik III's proclamation contains symbols of power, fame and wealth, but also of learning and the ability to divine the right course. If the picture was painted after Frederik's death (9 February 1670), it could

5 Trompe l'Oeil with Breakfast Piece and Goblets

1672
Oil on canvas, 132 x 183 cm
Copenhagen, Statens Museum for Kunst

The curtain has been pulled slightly aside to the right and one corner is turned up over the curtain cord. Light enters from the left to illuminate a still life arranged on a table covered with an oriental cloth and, on the left, also by a white napkin. The table-top is piled with a sumptuous breakfast piece of a lobster on a (Chinese?) porcelain dish; a ham placed on a metal-bound chest; a half-full rummer (or toasting cup), containing a peeled lemon; various fruits; a silver goblet borne by a Nereid and crowned by a Cupid and a gilt goblet topped by the figure of Fortuna.

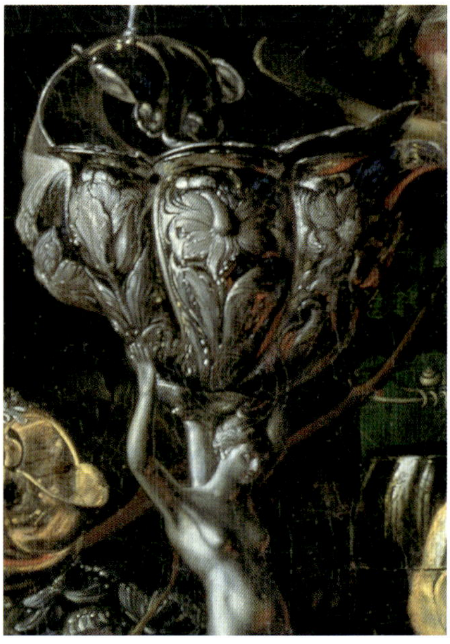

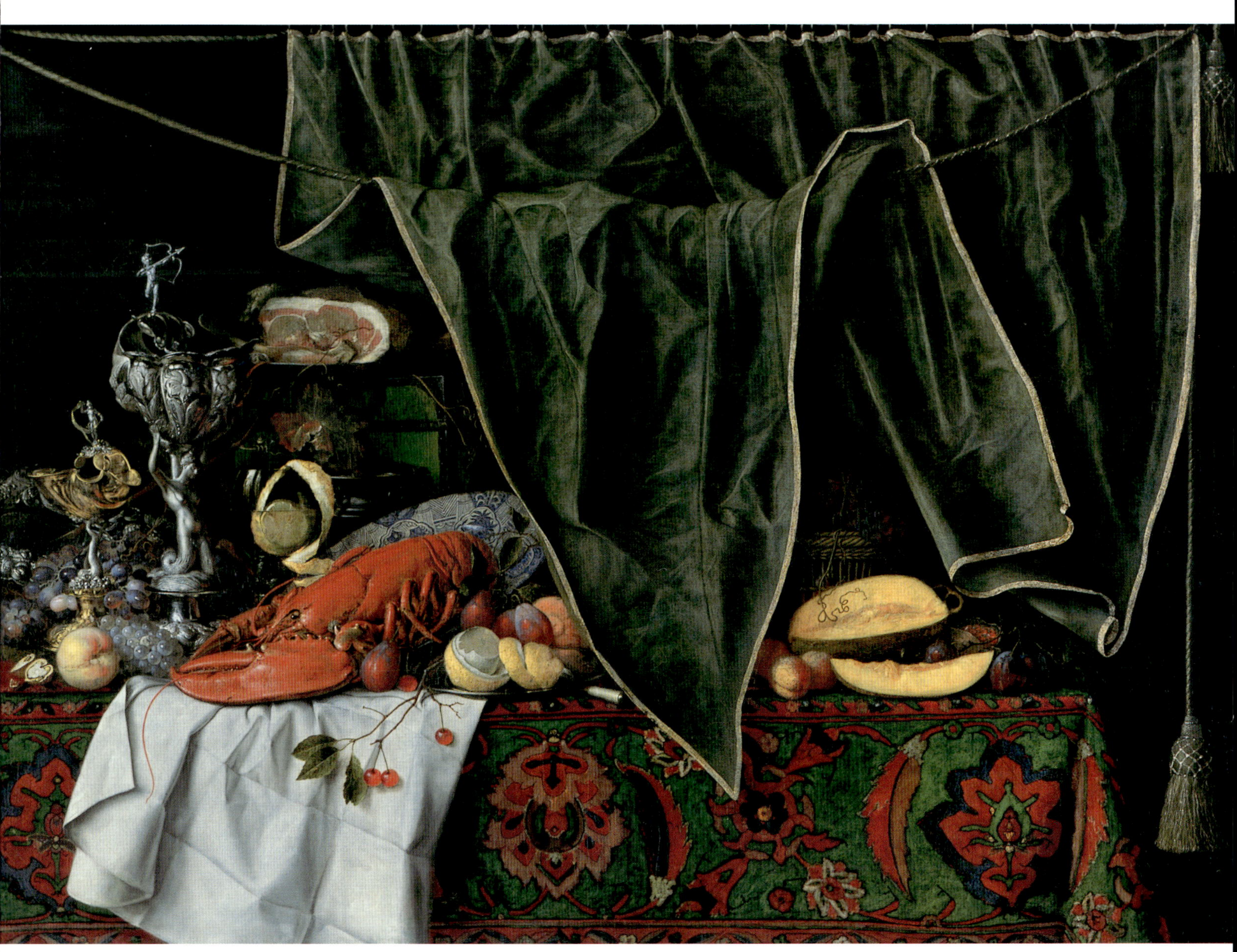

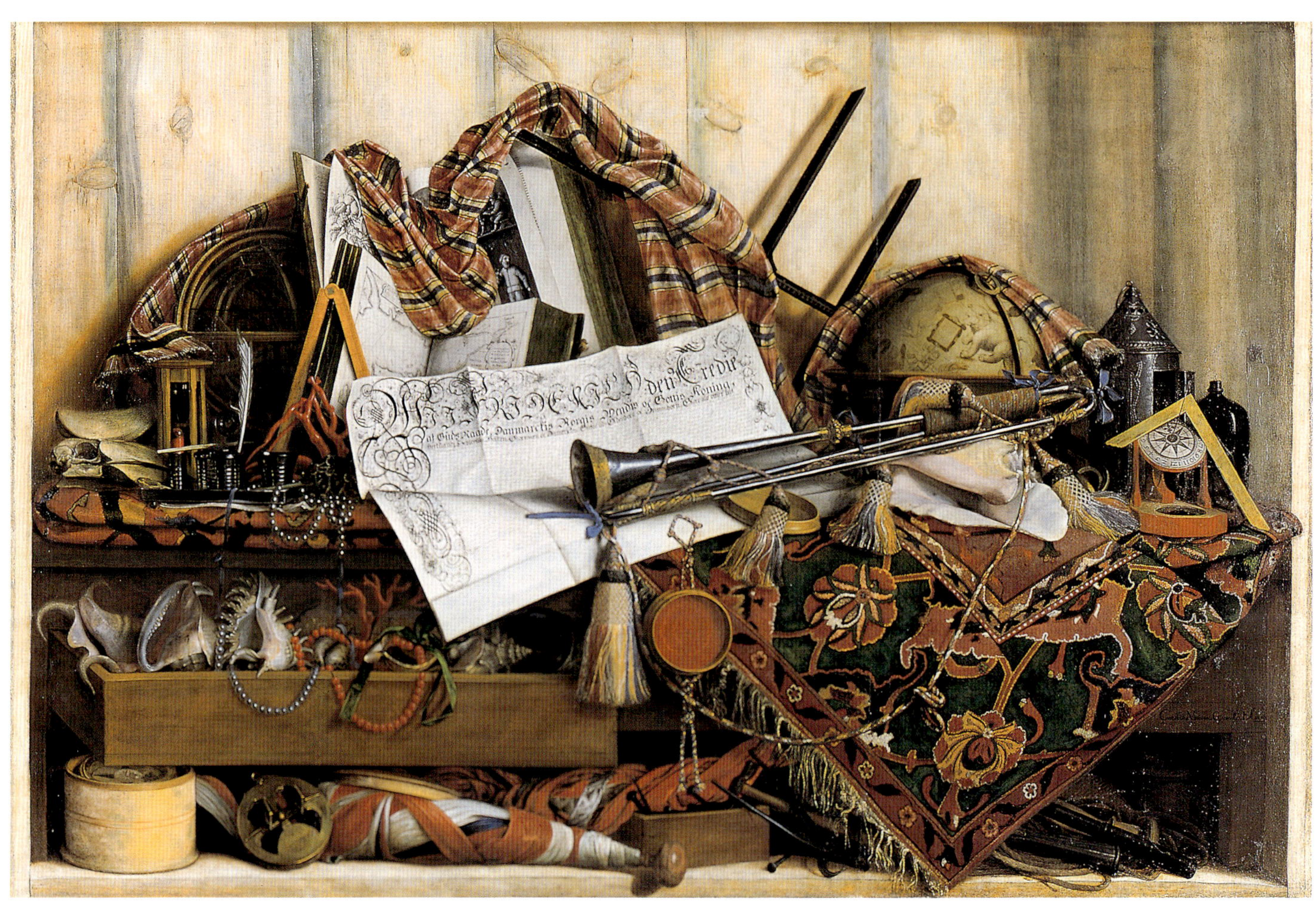

6 Trompe l'Oeil with Trumpet, Celestial Globe and Proclamation by Frederik III

1670
Oil on canvas, 132 x 201 cm
Copenhagen, Statens Museum for Kunst

A number of scientific and nautical instruments associated with a learned person are assembled on a bench in front of a wooden partition. On the right there is a cross-staff (for measuring the sun) and a celestial globe showing the constellations and signs of the zodiac. A book and another larger volume are propped up, open, against the partition. A trumpet decorated with tassels and braiding is placed partly on the proclamation of Frederik III, seemingly the central motif to the composition. The many scientific instruments, books and natural specimens contain references to the king as a scholarly collector in the arts and sciences. The picture appears to be a glorification of Frederik III and was probably painted after his death.

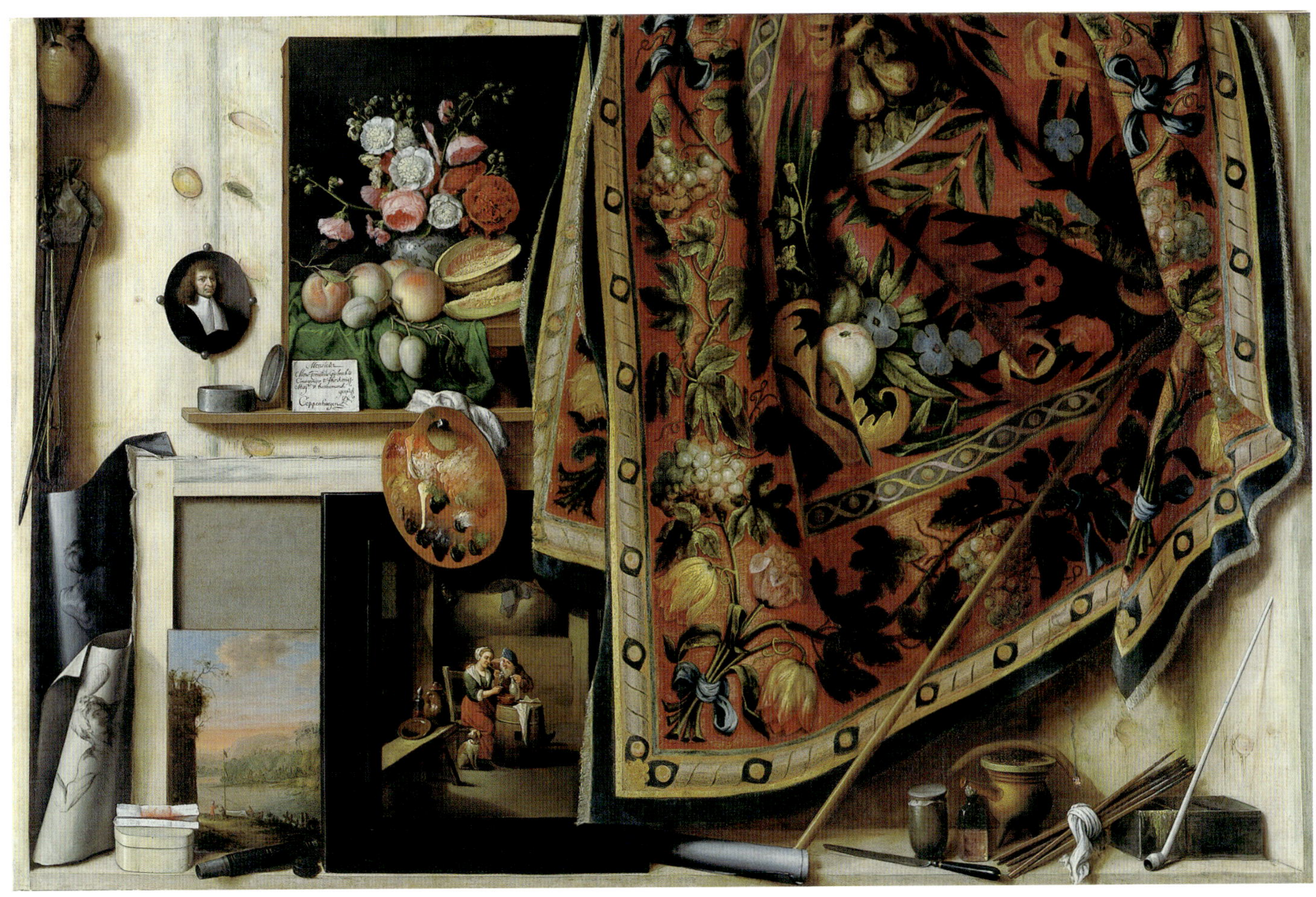

7 Trompe l'Oeil. Paintings, Painter's Tools and a Flower-Patterned Table-Cover in the Artist's Studio

Probably about 1670-72
Oil on canvas, 132 x 199 cm
Copenhagen, Statens Museum for Kunst

The picture represents a still life consisting of paintings, drawings and painter's tools against the background of a light board partition. Several pictures can be seen, including a genre scene in the style of David Teniers in a broad black frame, an unframed river landscape and a canvas mounted on a stretcher with the back facing out which is leaning against the wall under a shelf. The artist's maulstick rests against the curtain and below this is, amongst other things, a palette knife and a bundle of brushes. The picture is probably a companion piece to cat. no. **6**. The curtain suspended on the right is a Dutch seventeenth-century table-cover, which may be that known to have been in the possession of King Frederik III. The oval portrait on the left is a self portrait of Gijsbrechts, (see detail on page 13).

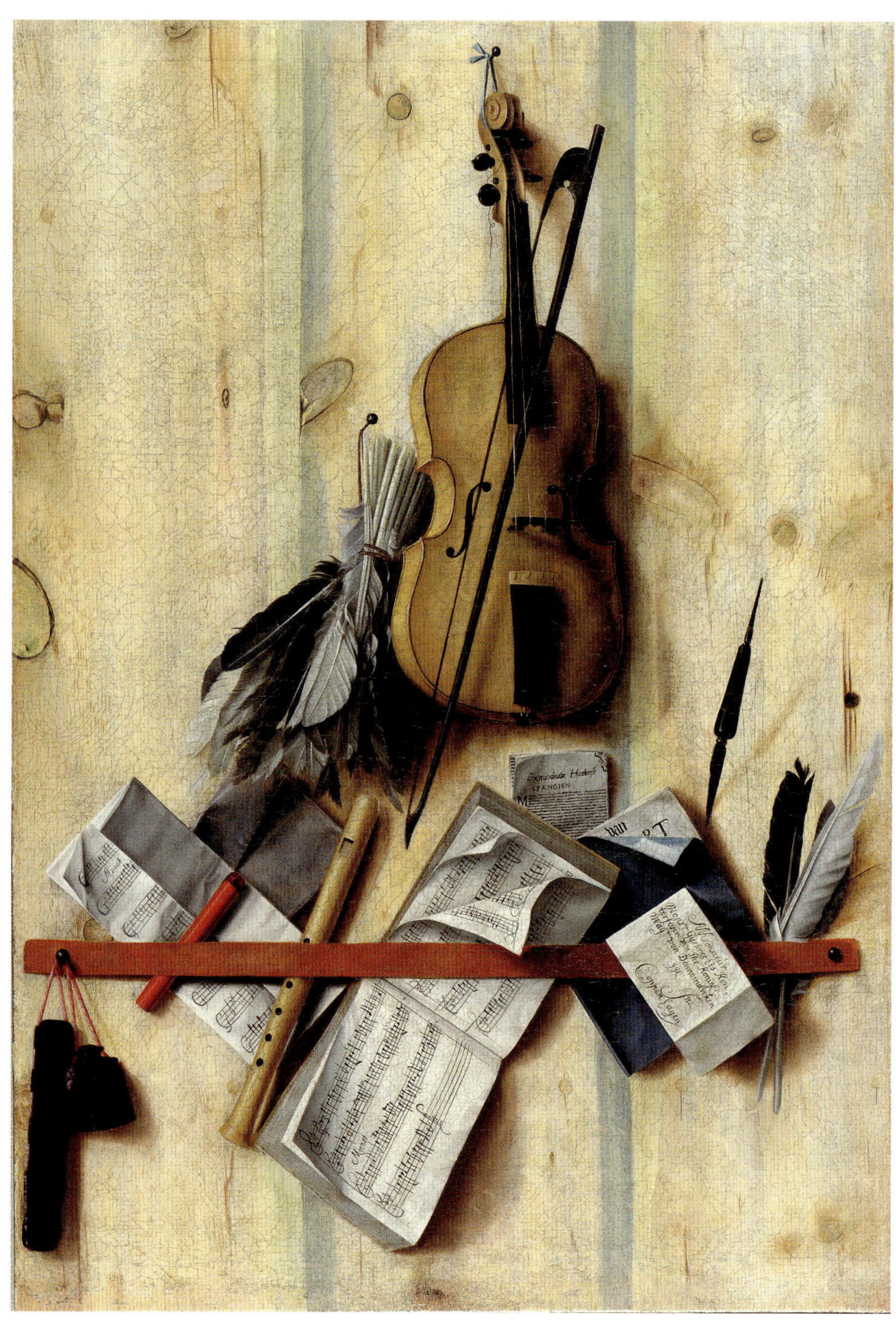

8 Trompe l'Oeil with Violin, Music Book and Recorder

Probably about 1672
Oil on canvas, 117 x 80 cm
Copenhagen, Statens Museum for Kunst

Here a combination of musical instruments, letters and writing implements are arranged against bare boards. Sheets of music, a recorder, an open book of music, the newspaper '*Oprechte Haerlemse Courant*', a letter addressed to Gijsbrechts in Copenhagen (detail, *below*), some quill pens and other objects are pushed behind one leather tape fixed across the board. On a nail above there is a violin with a bow, and beside it a bundle of quill pens. A penknife has been pushed into the board, throwing a long shadow across the surface of the wood. At the bottom left a quill-pen holder and a bottle of ink hang from the leather strap.

be thought of as a painted *laudatio funebris* (funeral eulogy). The other picture represents the world of art, in which genre painting, landscapes, still lifes and the human figure are all included. Actual *vanitas* motifs are not emphasised in the two pictures – the Frederik III picture includes an hourglass, and the studio picture a pipe-lighter and clay pipe. Together the pictures constitute a painted *Kunstkammer* of works of art, natural specimens and scientific instruments, one providing a 'self portrait' of the artist and the other a glorification of his royal patron. Starting in 1670 there are payments to Gijsbrechts in Christian V's private accounts for paintings executed for the king; these show that between 21 February 1670 and 1 April 1672 five payments were authorised.[35] On account of their summary nature it is not possible in general to link payments to specific pictures; it is nevertheless tempting to surmise that 600 *rigsdaler* authorised in payment for two pictures at the beginning of 1671 – over twice the largest amount in the accounts for a single picture – might be the payment for these two companion pieces.

Studio Walls

IN ANOTHER TYPE of trompe-l'oeil still life, the earliest known example of which is from 1663, Gijsbrechts reproduces a bare board partition (cat. no. 8). Sometimes this is set in his studio, and one of his own pictures is placed on a shelf, which acts as a kind of easel. On the shelf there are, typically, painter's tools such as a bundle of brushes and a small paint box spattered with oil paint, and under the shelf a palette, a cloth and a bottle of oil or the like. On the board partition surrounding the picture, there might be some small oval portraits, sometimes a self portrait, and, at the top, a knife inserted between the picture and the board or between the canvas and the stretcher. A recently completed picture on a stretcher is on the shelf, but the canvas has detached itself from the stretcher at a top corner and hangs

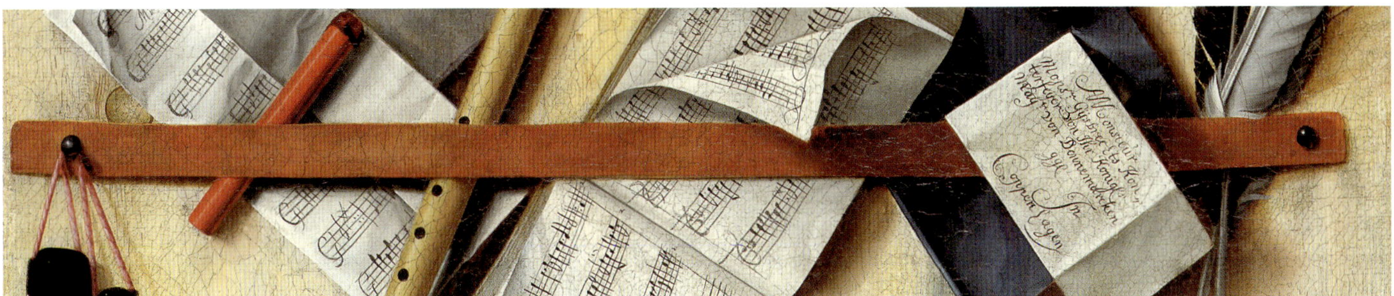

down revealing its reverse. This idea of the turned-down canvas does seem to be an original invention, but did at least have a forerunner: *A Vision of the Holy Family Near Verona* (*fig. 8*), dated 1581 and attributed to Battista Angolo del Moro (active late sixteenth century), depicts an evening view of Verona, but the top edge of the canvas has been illusionistically 'rolled down' to reveal beneath it a painting of the Holy Family, which, in addition, can even be made out *through* the canvas in front.

In a picture from 1664, now in Hull (cat. no. 9), Gijsbrechts is progressing towards the final form of his studio wall as described above – a *vanitas* still life with skull, burned-down candle, hourglass and soap bubbles stands on a shelf. There is also a palette, bundle of brushes, and paint box daubed with paint. At the edge of the detached canvas hanging down over the picture we can see loose threads, flaps of canvas and holes left by nails. There is a small oval portrait of an unidentified man fixed to the stretcher, and a knife has been stuck in horizontally between canvas and stretcher. The wall is only visible as a narrow strip around the picture on the shelf.

Perhaps the most important example of this type of trompe l'oeil is the *Studio Wall and Vanitas Still Life* in Copenhagen, dated 1668 (cat. no. 10). The *vanitas*

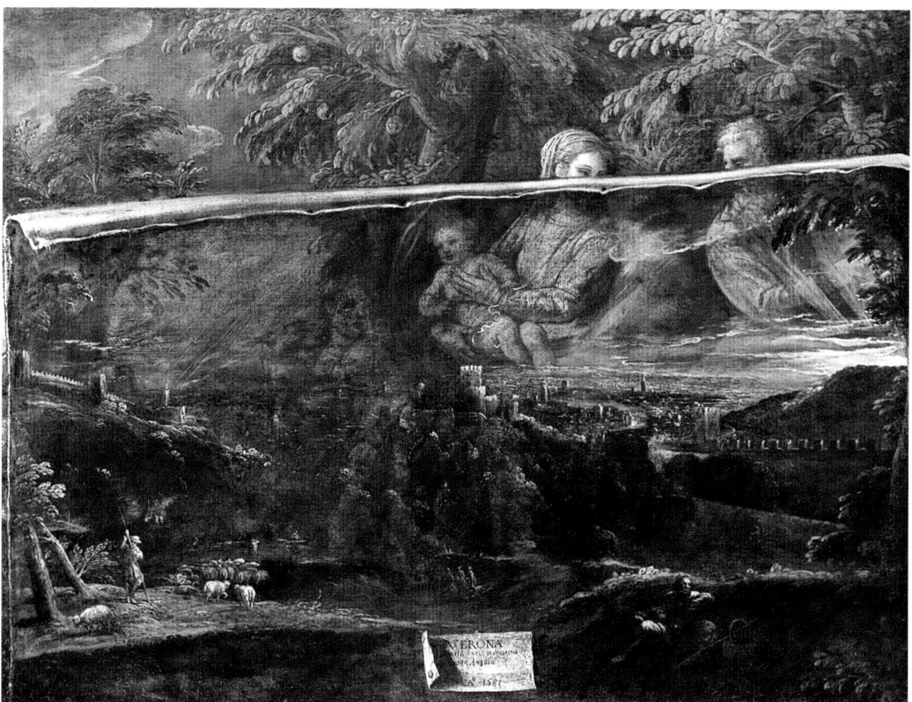

9 Trompe l'Oeil Studio Wall with Vanitas Still Life

1664
Oil on canvas, 87 x 70 cm
Kingston upon Hull, Ferens Art Gallery

The *vanitas* still life is propped up on a shelf in the artist's studio together with the artist's palette, brushes and paint box. The paint on the palette is still wet, the yellow and yellow-pink, in particular, dripping in a thick mass. The *vanitas* picture contains familiar symbols about the ephemeral nature of temporal things and the inevitability of death. For example, the violin and wine glass represent enjoyment and riches; the proclamation by the authorities and the pistol represent temporal power. The hourglass, the pocket watch, the candlestick with burned-down candle, the soap bubbles and the skull, all refer to the transitory nature of life. The skull with its wreath of corn symbolises the Christian hope of resurrection. The top corner of the canvas has become detached from the stretcher and is hanging down over the picture. The motif is of the illusion, broken – literally coming away from the painted surface of the picture.

Fig. 8

Battista Angelo del Moro (?)
A Vision of the Holy Family near Verona
1581
Oil on canvas, 90 x 117 cm
Oberlin, Ohio. Allen Memorial Art Museum, Oberlin College

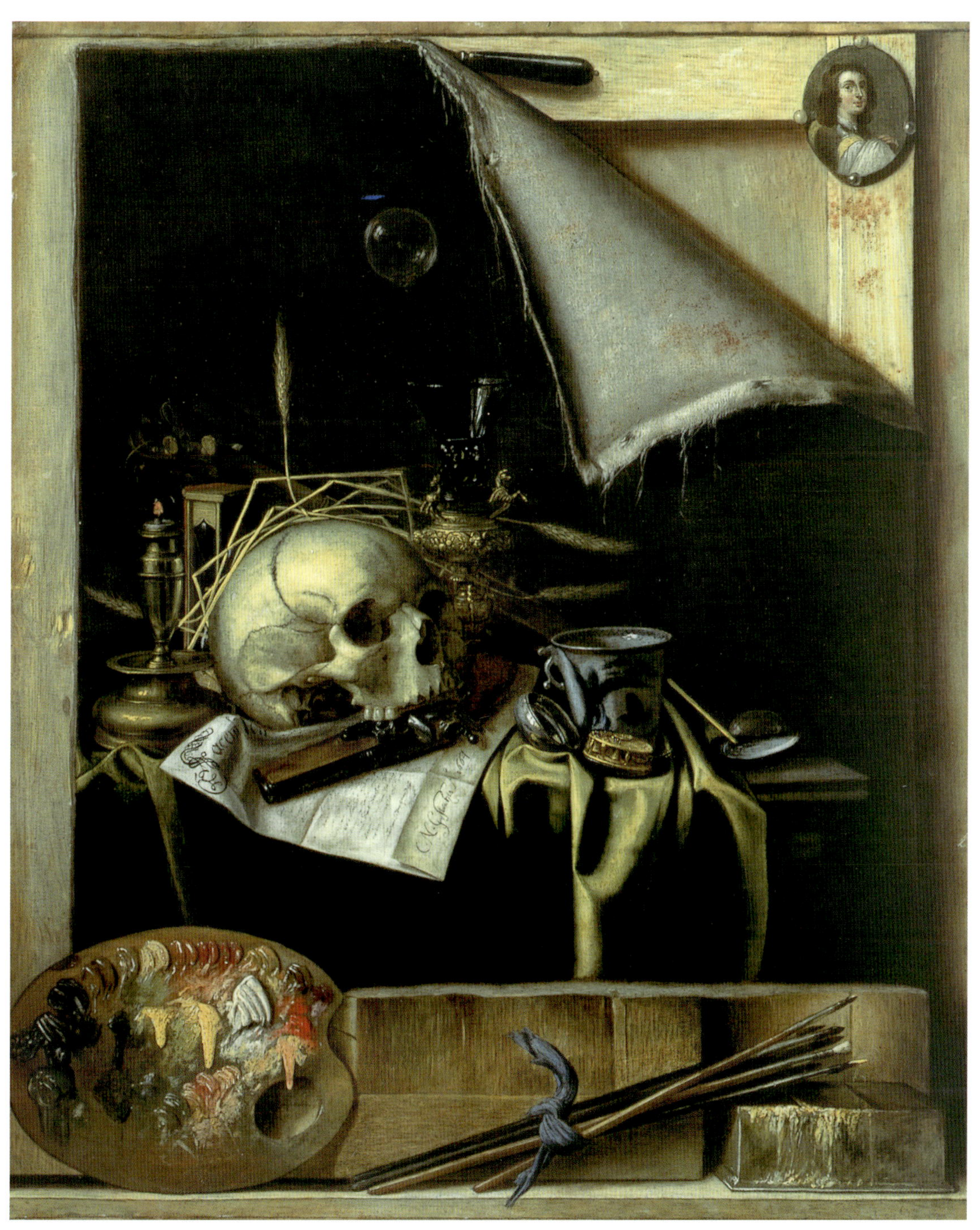

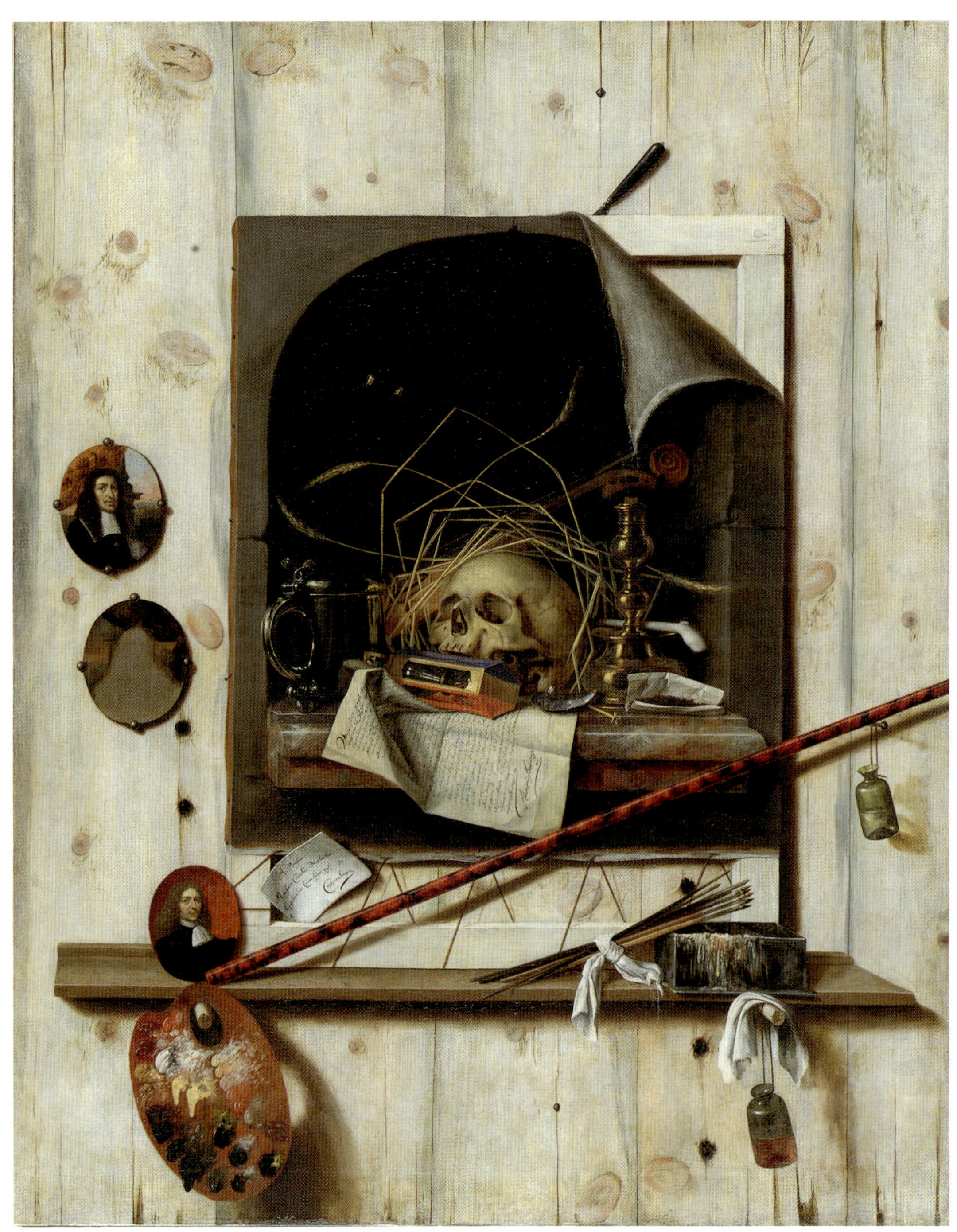

10 Trompe l'Oeil with Studio Wall and Vanitas Still Life

1668

Oil on canvas, 152 x 118 cm

Copenhagen, Statens Museum for Kunst

A *vanitas* still life on canvas, with its bottom edge laced onto a stretcher, leans on a shelf in the artist's studio surrounded by his tools and three small oval portraits. Two oval portraits are tacked to the wall, one is a is a portrait of an unidentified person and the other a mysterious, almost blank, canvas. Another portrait is propped up on the shelf against the stretcher and board partition. The partition is executed with the utmost attention to detail to show the knots, splinters and blue-rot and other peculiarities of pinewood.

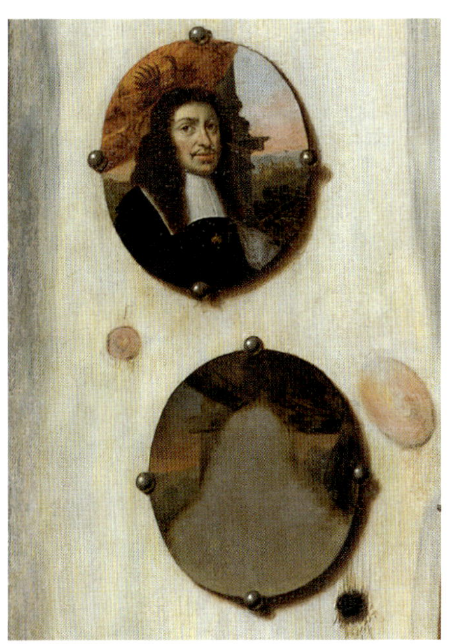

picture is on a stretcher, with strings through the canvas at the bottom, and is standing on a shelf. It is surrounded by artist's tools and three small oval portraits, two of which are nailed to the board partition. The one at the top represents the Emperor Leopold I (1640–1705) wearing the insignia of the Golden Fleece.[36] The portrait below is no more than an outline waiting to be filled with the right person, presumably at the discretion of the client. The final portrait, leaning against the base of the stretcher, cannot be identified – it is tempting to see it as a self portrait, but the image does not resemble other suggested self portraits by Gijsbrechts. The work is composed strictly along horizontal and vertical lines which, however, are broken by striking diagonals, dominated by the red, marbled maulstick. The picture on the shelf is a beautiful and powerful *vanitas* containing all the familiar symbols of the transience of life standing on a marble sill in a niche: life is short (the hour-glass), evanescent as smoke (the pipe and the tobacco), it runs out like the candle burning down, like the dying tones or fragile strings of the violin. Human life is frail and ephemeral like a soap bubble. Death is inevitable (the skull), but the wreath of corn around the skull symbolises resurrection after death. Just as the corn is buried and then bursts into renewed life, the same will happen for mankind too: '*Mors vitae initium*', 'Death is the beginning of life'. The illusionistically painted niche gives the picture a solemn, sacral character, and in early still-life painting the motif of a niche also seems to have been used frequently in connection with *vanitas* themes. The same *vanitas* accessories are also found in the picture in Hull (cat. no. 9) and in both works we also see the bent canvas with threads at its edge – initially, of course, to trick us into trying to lift it up and fix it back on the stretcher, but also to tell us that the depiction of reality, which itself is a deception, is not a perpetuation of this reality, but merely a piece of canvas that will vanish like everything else. The studio wall is the artist's own reminder that art, too, is subject to the law of transience.

In another picture in Copenhagen (cat. no. 11), Gijsbrechts has put an illusionistically painted canvas up on a wall, almost as he does in his studio walls, but in this case without a stretcher or shelf. On the canvas he has painted two birds hanging on a wall. The top left corner of the canvas has detached itself from the wall and is very frayed at the edges. This picture within a picture is not painted quite to the edge of the canvas, and the artist has depicted the weave of the uncovered canvas as well as the reddish-brown underpainting. The birds in the picture are painted quite crudely, possibly only sketched, without any attempt at a trompe-l'oeil effect, possibly with the intention of emphasising the character of the still life as a piece of painted canvas, in contrast to the carefully painted boards.

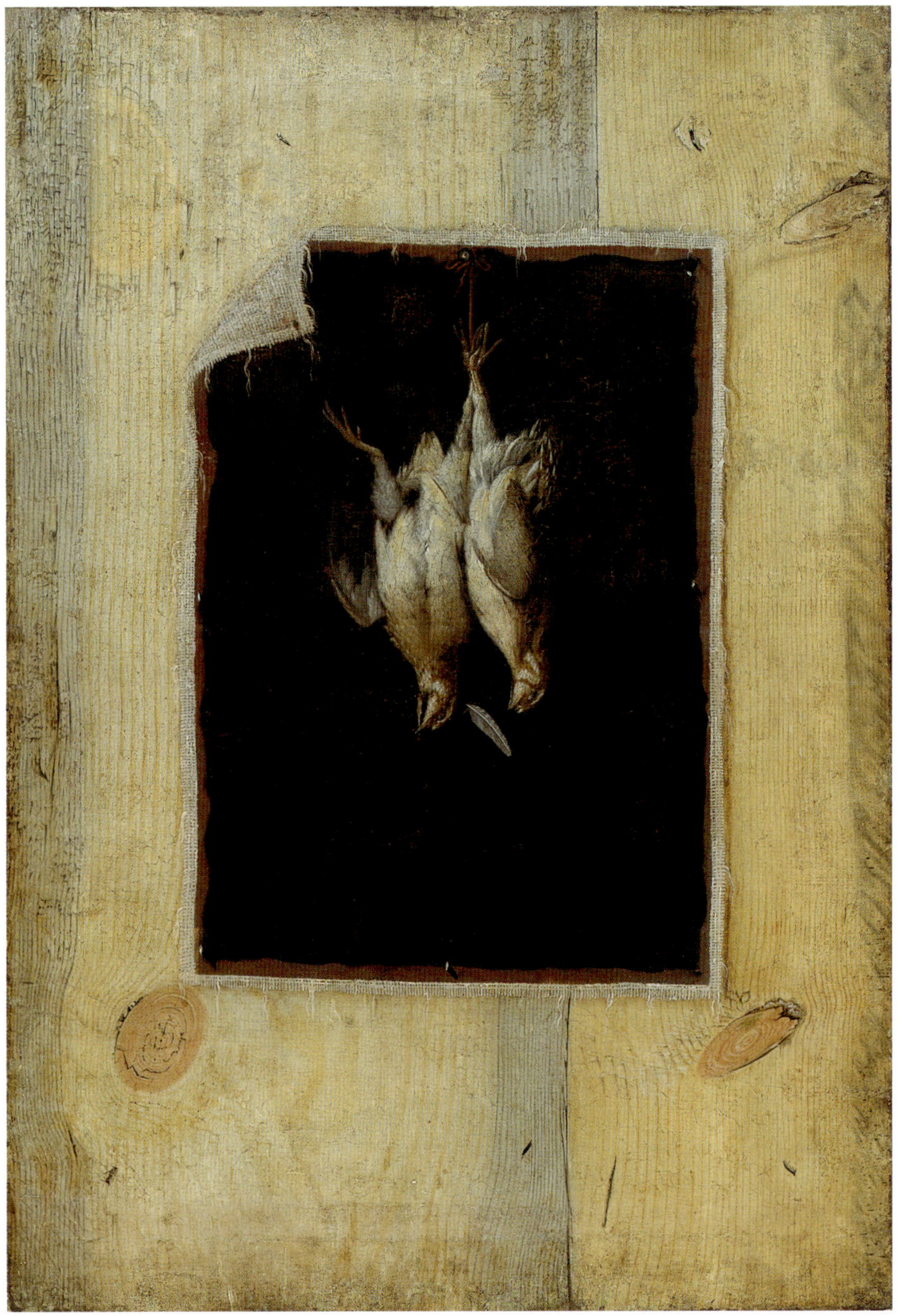

11 Trompe l'Oeil. Still Life of Two Dead Birds Hanging on a Wall

1670/72
Oil on canvas, 77 x 52.2 cm
Copenhagen, Statens Museum for Kunst

Like the Studio Walls with *vanitas* still lives or fruit pieces, this painting is a depiction of a picture within a picture. Here, however, Gijsbrechts has dispensed with the stretcher and simply mounted the unstretched canvas on a partition wall. A corner of the canvas has come away from the wall and hangs down over the picture, revealing its unpainted and frayed underside. The edges of the canvas are not painted, allowing the artist the opportunity to paint the trompe-l'oeil weave of the bare canvas and to show the picture's reddish-brown underpainting. The birds conversely are painted without any attempt at a trompe l'oeil effect, possibly to accentuate the character of the picture as a piece of painted canvas.

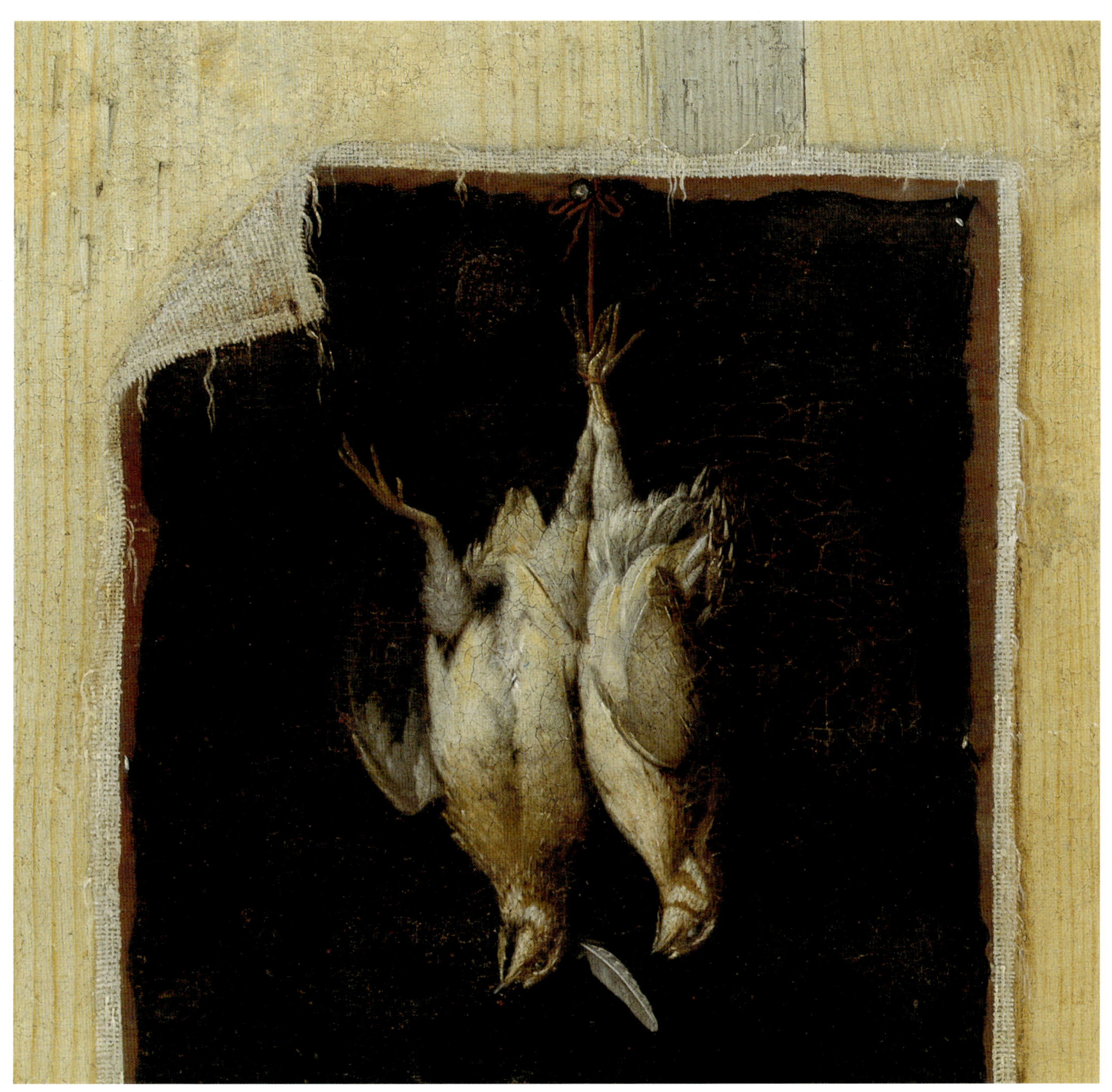

Trompe-l'oeil Cupboards

THE WALL CUPBOARD as a trompe-l'oeil motif and the closely related motif of the niche were apparently known in Antiquity, and became increasingly common in European art during the Renaissance. Two illusionistically painted niches or open cupboards fitted with shelves and containing liturgical objects are painted at the base of the eastern wall of Taddeo Gaddi's (active 1320s-1366) frescoes from

Figs. 9 and 9a

Taddeo Gaddi
Cupboard with vessels and
Cupboard with book
1328–30
Fresco
Florence, Baroncelli Chapel, Santa Croce

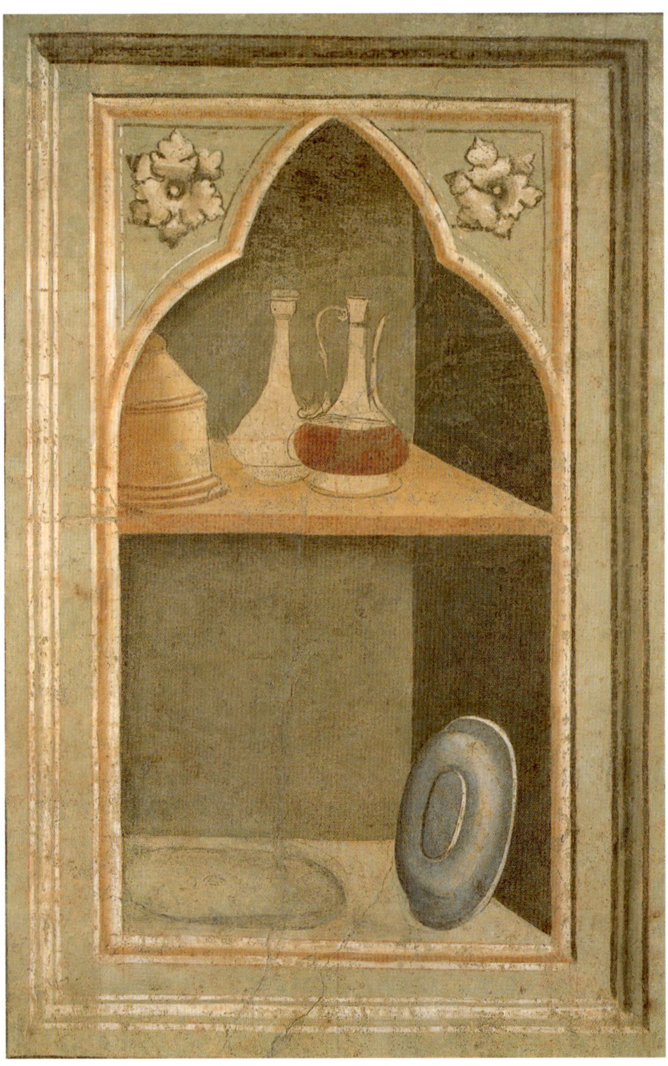

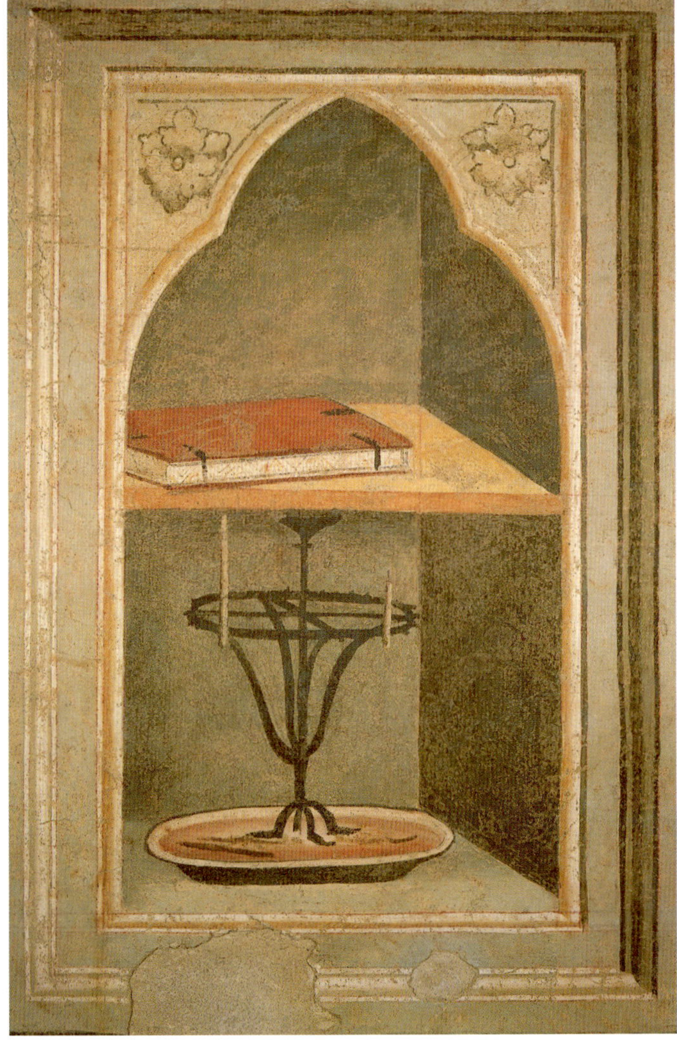

Samuel van Hoogstraten
A Bearded Man at a Window
1653
Oil on canvas, 111 x 85.5 cm
Vienna, Kunsthistorisches Museum

Samuel van Hoogstraten
Trompe l'Oeil Cabinet Door with Still life
1655
oil on canvas, 92.3 x 72.2 cm
Vienna, Gemäldegalerie der Akademie der bildenden Künste

1328–30 in the Baroncelli Chapel in Santa Croce in Florence (*figs. 9 and 9a*),[37] but the motif became particularly popular during the Italian Renaissance in the *intarsia* (mosaic woodwork) decoration created for churches and *studioli* (little studies) in princely palaces. One of the most important *studioli* is that which Francesco di Giorgio Martini (1439–1501) and Baccio Pontelli (1450– after November 1494) created in the 1470s for Federigo II di Montefeltro, Duke of Urbino, in the ducal palace at Urbino. The *intarsia* decoration on the walls here consists of illusionistic cupboards with half-open doors, behind which are objects such as musical instruments, books, armour and scientific instruments.

As an independent motif in painting, the illusionistic open cupboard without a door was taken up at the beginning of the seventeenth century by the German painter Georg Flegel (*fig. 2*). There can be no doubt, however, that Gijsbrechts derived the inspiration for his wall cupboards from Samuel van Hoogstraten, who had created illusionistically painted wall cupboards and windows in Vienna and Regensburg in the first half of the 1650s in such pictures as *A Bearded Man at a Window*, dated 1653 (*fig. 10*), and a *Cabinet Door with Still Life* (*fig. 11*).[38]

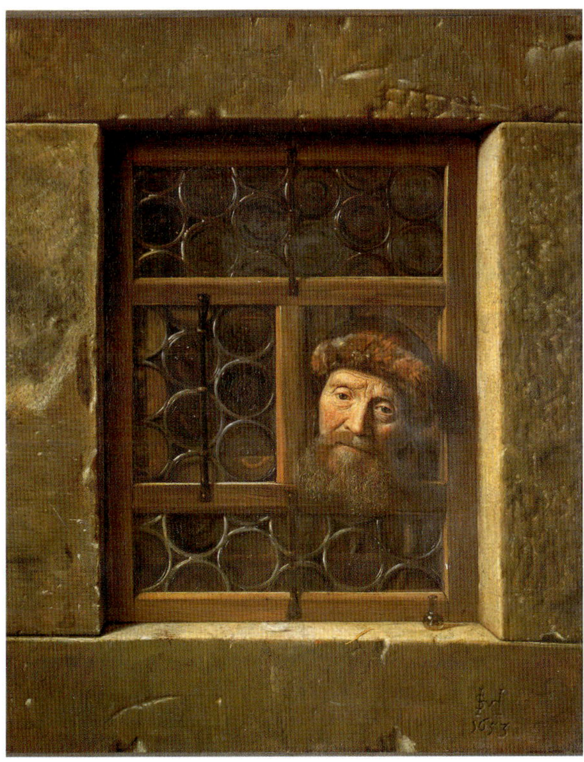

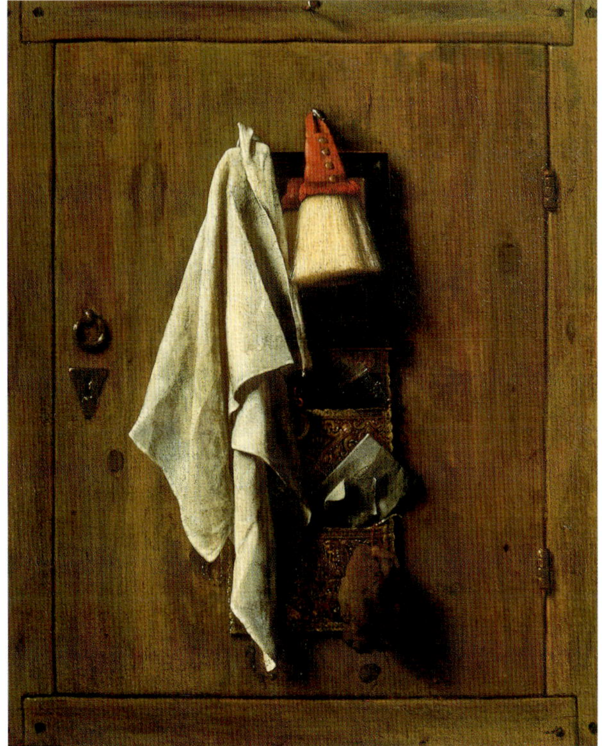

Gijsbrechts's trompe-l'oeil cupboards are usually on almost square canvases, composed of an illusionistic depiction of the front of a cupboard with a door hinged on a broad frame imitating pinewood. The surface of the picture represents the front of the cupboard, the door of which can be closed or open. As a kind of display cabinet, the cupboard has a window with leaded panes, some of which may be broken. Various letters, printed sheets and other objects are pushed down either behind an iron bar fixed across the window or under the window frame and the lead bars around the glass panes. Through the glass, the contents of the cupboard can be seen – the illusion therefore is both behind and in front of the surface of the actual picture. Gijsbrechts painted only a small number of trompe-l'oeil pictures of this type. The earliest dated one is in Rouen (cat. no. 12), and represents a closed wall cupboard, with several of the leaded panes of the glass door broken or cracked. Some letters, a quill pen, a song book containing '*Zwey schön newe / Weltliche Lieder*' (Two new profane songs), a comb and a bundle of landscape prints – the foremost of which bears Gijsbrechts's name and is dated 1665 – have all been pushed down behind or hang over the iron bar fixed horizontally across the window. There are other letters and a printed sheet fixed in the bars behind the panes. Apart from a letter pushed down in the left-hand corner of the frame, the objects in the window are symmetrically distributed in a festoon-like pattern. The key in the cupboard lock, the sealed letter at the bottom left and the quill pen throw bold shadows onto the window frame.

12 Trompe l'Oeil of a Closed Cupboard

1665
Oil on canvas, 69 x 59 cm
Rouen, Musées des Beaux-Arts

A closed wall cabinet has leaded panes in the door, the top row of which are semi-circular and through which two closed drawers can be seen. Several of the glass panes have been broken. Some letters, a quill pen, a songbook, a comb and a bundle of landscape prints have been pushed down behind the bar across the window. Other letters and a printed booklet are fixed in the bars behind the panes. Gijsbrechts is given ample opportunity for displaying his mastery of trompe-l'oeil effects, for instance in the papers inside and outside the cabinet and the key in the lock (detail *left*).

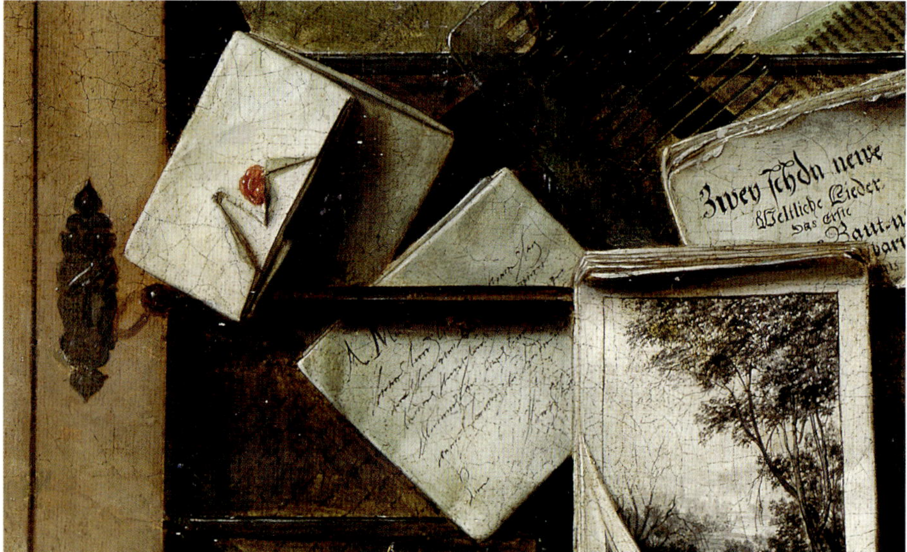

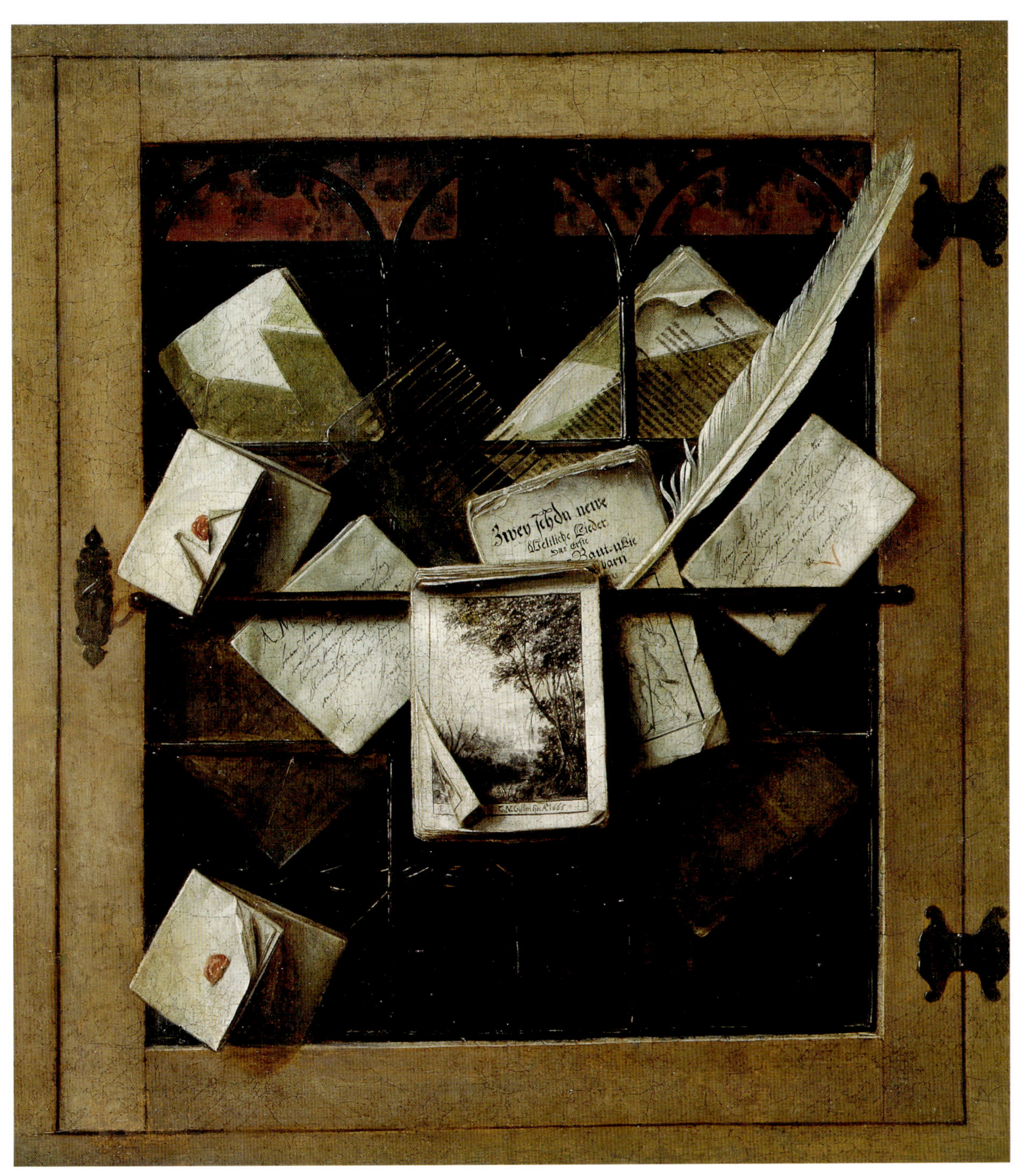

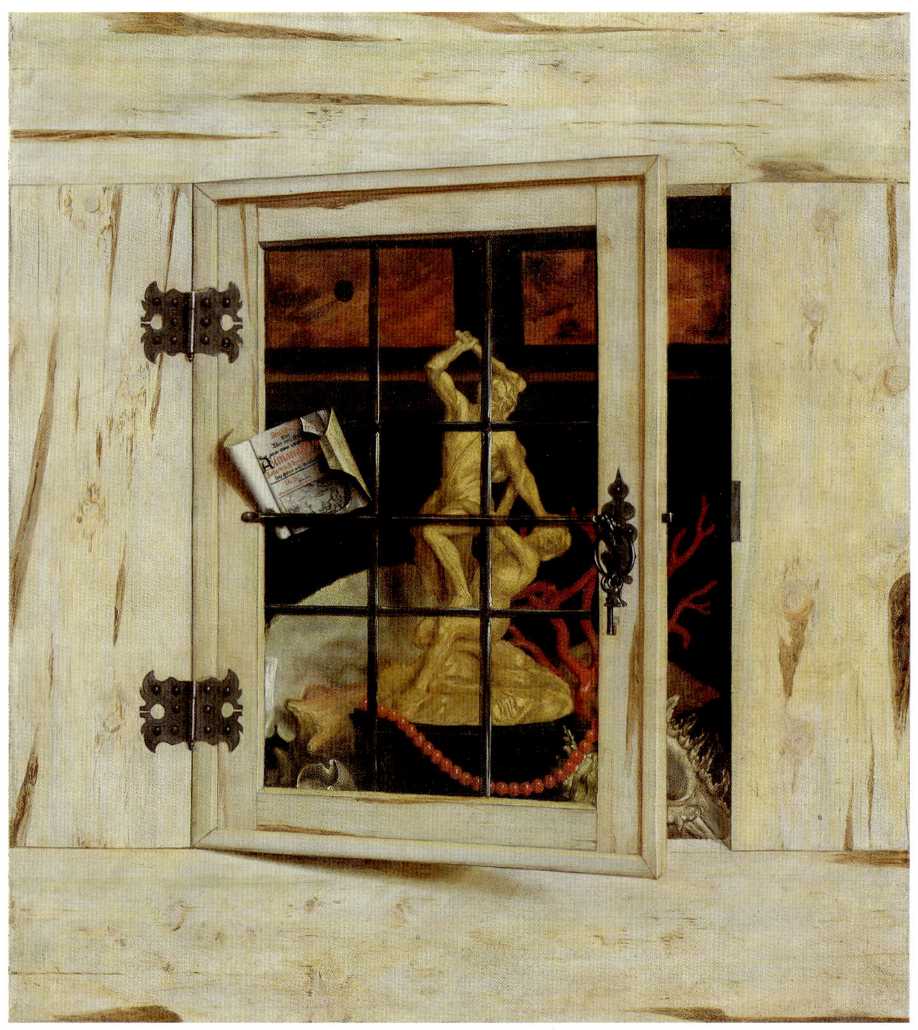

1670
Oil on canvas, 99.5 x 89.5 cm
Copenhagen, Statens Museum for Kunst

The illusionistically painted wall cabinet, with its leaded-paned door ajar, is hinged to a broad pinewood frame. An open almanac for the year 1670 is pushed in behind the iron bar across the middle of the door. Two keys and a signet stamp are in the lock and the overall impression is that the door has just been opened to reveal a pearlised, exotic looking shell and some raw coral. Encouraged by the light, which enters the picture from the right, the viewer glimpses a statuette group of *Hercules and the Vices* and a coral necklace through the glass. A similar statuette to this one, made in boxwood by the German ivory carver Joachim Henne, was once in a collection of valuables belonging to Frederik III in the 1660s. Today it is preserved in the Rosenborg Palace.

Two later trompe-l'oeil cupboards painted in Copenhagen are companion pieces. In one (cat. no. 13), the cupboard door, which is ajar, is hinged on the left and the light falls from the right, while in the other (cat. no. 14) the door, which is closed, is hinged on the right and the light enters from the left. The two pictures are different in several respects from the Rouen cupboard: to begin with, the artist has made much of the reproduction of the solid pinewood frames; secondly, only a small number of letters, documents and other objects have been pushed in behind or are hanging over the iron bar in front of the leaded panes. This makes it easier to see the natural specimens and artefacts in the cupboard.

14 Trompe l'Oeil. A Cabinet of Curiosities with an Ivory Tankard

1670
Oil on canvas, 99.5 x 89.5 cm
Copenhagen, Statens Museum for Kunst

Unlike its companion piece, (cat. no. **13**), the hinges and the lock on this cabinet are not an illusion and the door actually opens, just as the lock can be turned by the key. Behind the iron bar are letters, a quill pen and the newspaper *Oprechte Haerlemse*. Two of the leaded panes are broken and a letter and a penknife are squeezed in between the window frame and the pane. Inside the cupboard are a carved ivory tankard and a small figure of a horseman. The ivory tankard is carved with a depiction of the *Rape of the Sabine Women* and reproduces a similar piece by the German ivory carver, Joachim Henne. The reverse of the cupboard door (cat. no. **14a,** *below*) shows the 'backs' of objects seen through the 'front' of the door.

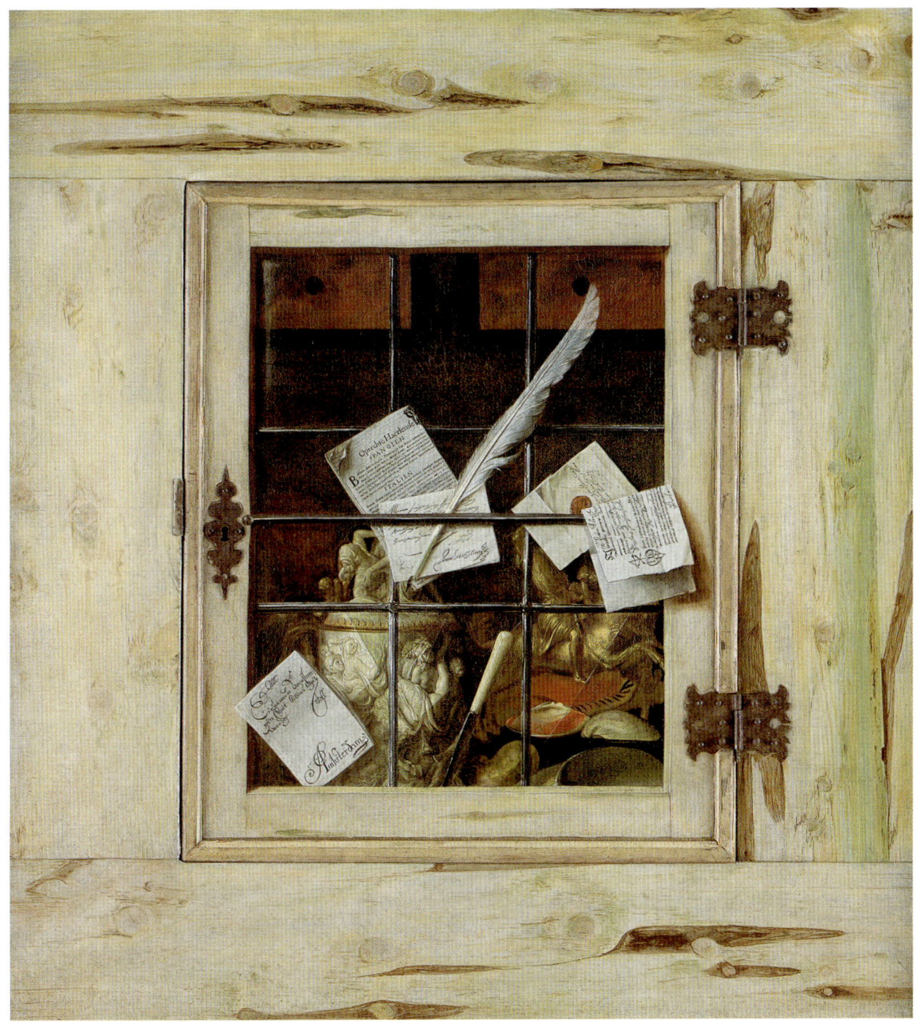

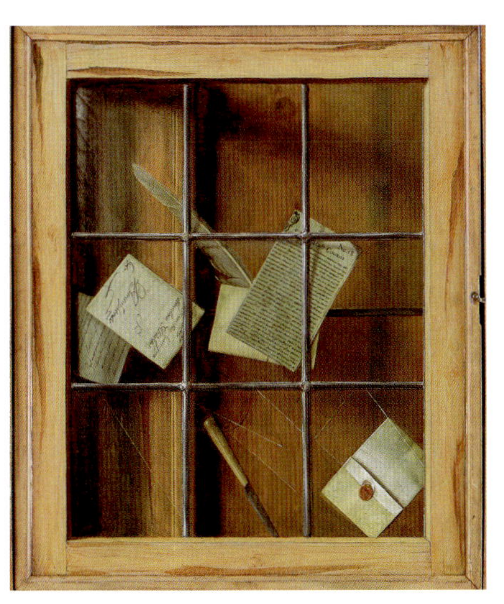

In his depiction of the closed cupboard (cat. no. 14), Gijsbrechts has taken a three-dimensional step to add new aspects to the trompe-l'oeil genre – the door of the cupboard can actually be opened. It turns on iron hinges fixed to the frame, and the lock, too, is a real metal lock that can be turned with a real key. On the reverse of the cupboard door, we can look through the back of its glass 'window' at the backs of the objects fixed to the front of the door. Beyond these we can see a wooden wall in the imaginary room in which the cupboard is placed. On the other hand, once the door has been opened, the contents of the cupboard itself, the artefacts and natural specimens, have disappeared, and we see only an empty frame.

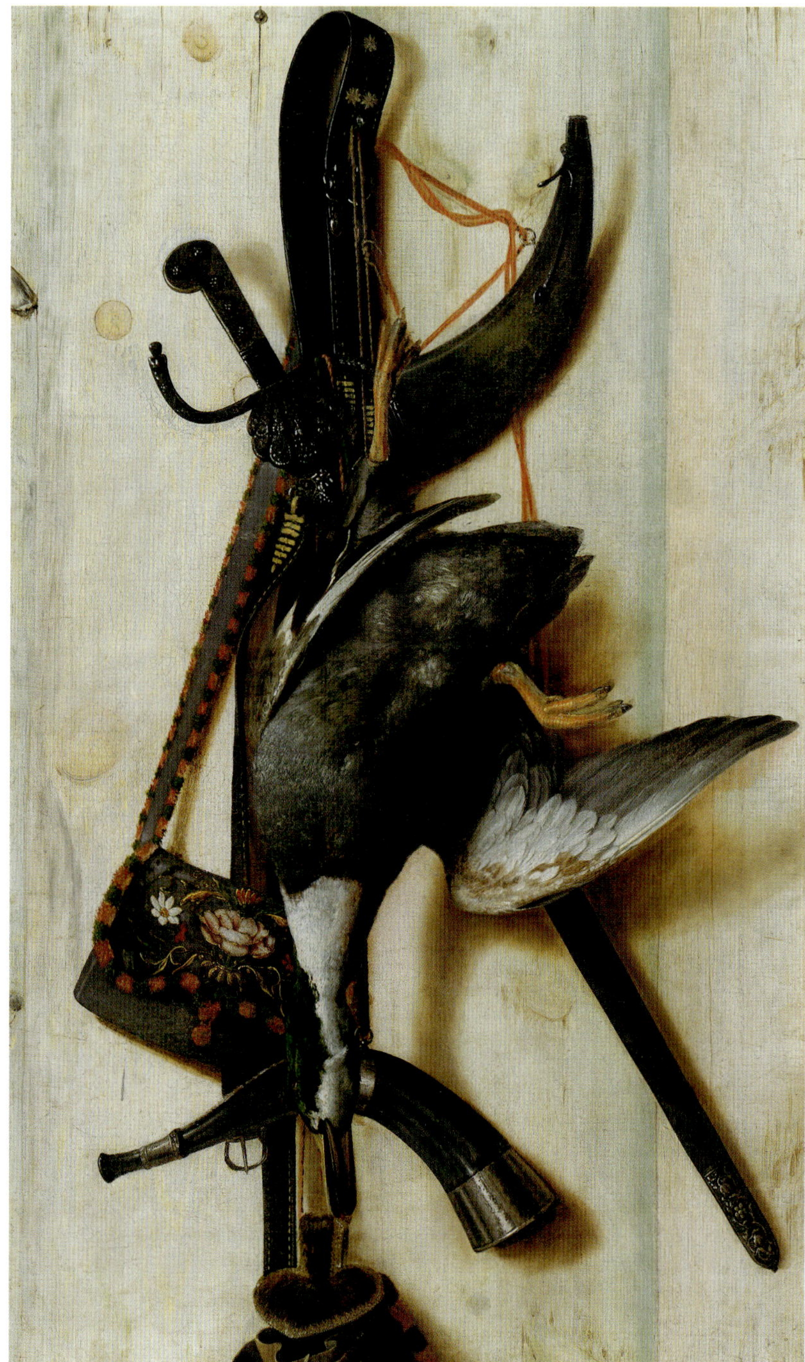

15 Trompe l'Oeil with a Dead Duck and Hunting Implements

Probably about 1670–72
Oil on canvas, 114.3 x 66.8 cm
Copenhagen, Statens Museum for Kunst

A dead duck, a hunting sword and strap, a hunting bag, a powder horn and what may be a pistol holster are hanging from a pinewood partition. The sword marks a striking diagonal in the otherwise predominantly vertical composition. The picture has almost certainly been cut on all four sides, seen most strikingly at the bottom where a hunting bag(?) is cut off by the edge of the picture. Light enters the picture from the left casting dark shadows on the light-coloured pinewood partition.

Trompe-l'oeil Still Lifes of Game and Hunting Implements

Below detail of cat. no **15**
The hunting bag with its embroidered flower motif and tasselled fringe-work contrasts beautifully with the bird's feathered head hanging lifelessly beside it. The curved powder horn with its metallic embellishments adds a further dimension to an area rich in the contrasts of textured surfaces.

AROUND 1650 A number of artists in Holland began painting trompe-l'oeil still lifes of game birds hanging from a nail on a board partition or monochrome wall.[39] This type of game piece can be found as early as the beginning of the sixteenth century with Jacopo de' Barbari's famous trompe-l'oeil still life from 1504, *Partridge, Iron Gloves and Crossbow Bolt* (fig. 1). Gijsbrechts did not go in for this popular trompe-l'oeil game piece to any great extent, although there is one tall, narrow picture (undoubtedly cut) of a dead duck hanging on a pine board, along with a hunting sword, powder horn and the like (cat. no. 15). Numerous trompe-l'oeil still lifes of such hunting implements on their own do, however, survive.

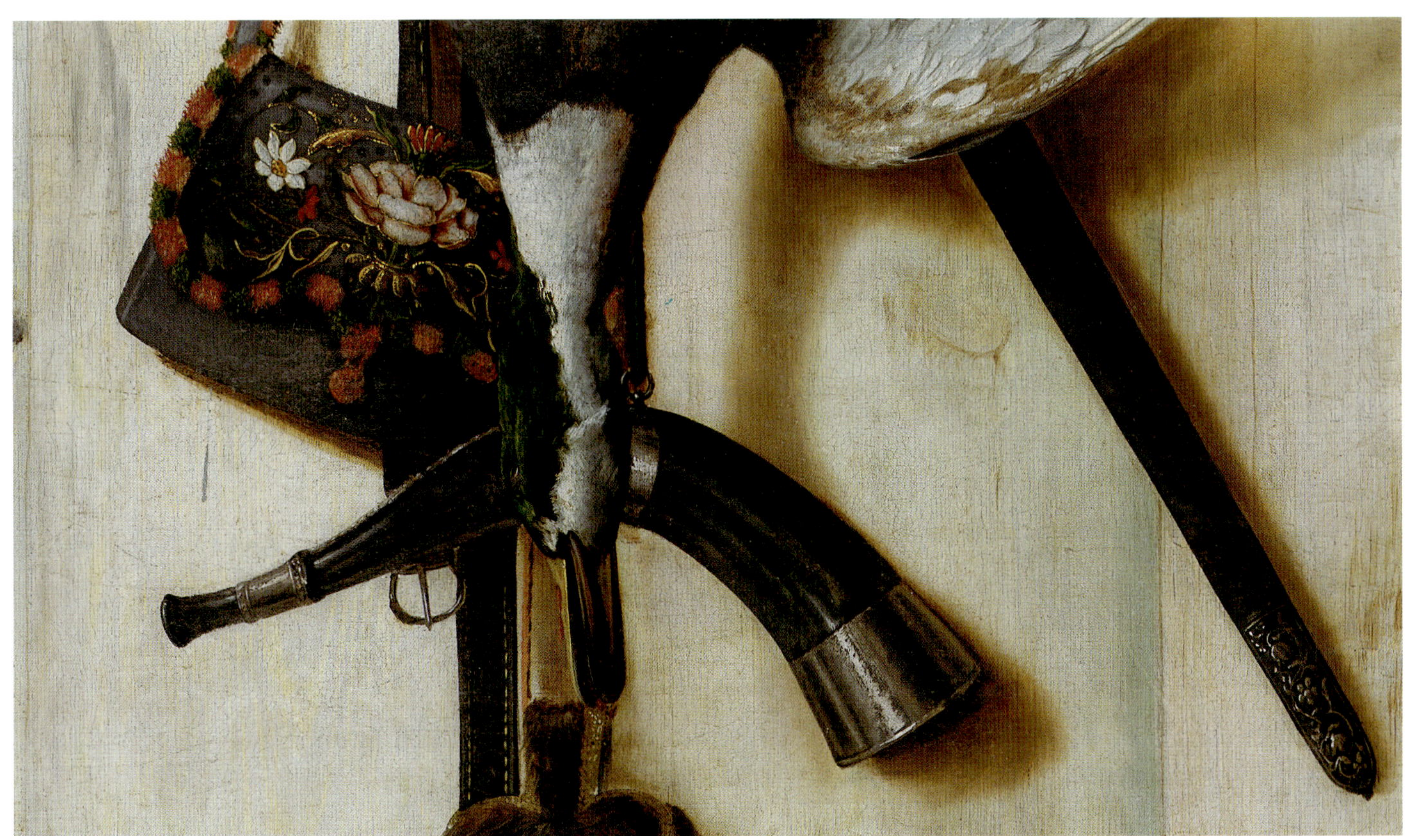

In a series of respectively four and two of such trompe-l'oeil still lifes in Copenhagen, Gijsbrechts reproduced a number of Christian V's own hunting implements, which are still preserved in Rosenborg Palace. In the first, *Trompe l'Oeil with Hunting Knife and Hunting Horn. Equipment for Riding to Hounds* (cat. no. 16) we see the King's hunting knife in a splendid gilt silver-mounted sheath decorated with hunting motifs and the monogram, 'C5',[40] in addition to a brass bugle and a hunting horn, the latter of which can still be seen at Rosenborg.[41] In *Trompe l'Oeil with Falconer's Bag and other Equipment for Falconry* (cat. no. 17), the artist has depicted a game bag, decoy and falcon's hood, all still at Rosenborg.[42]

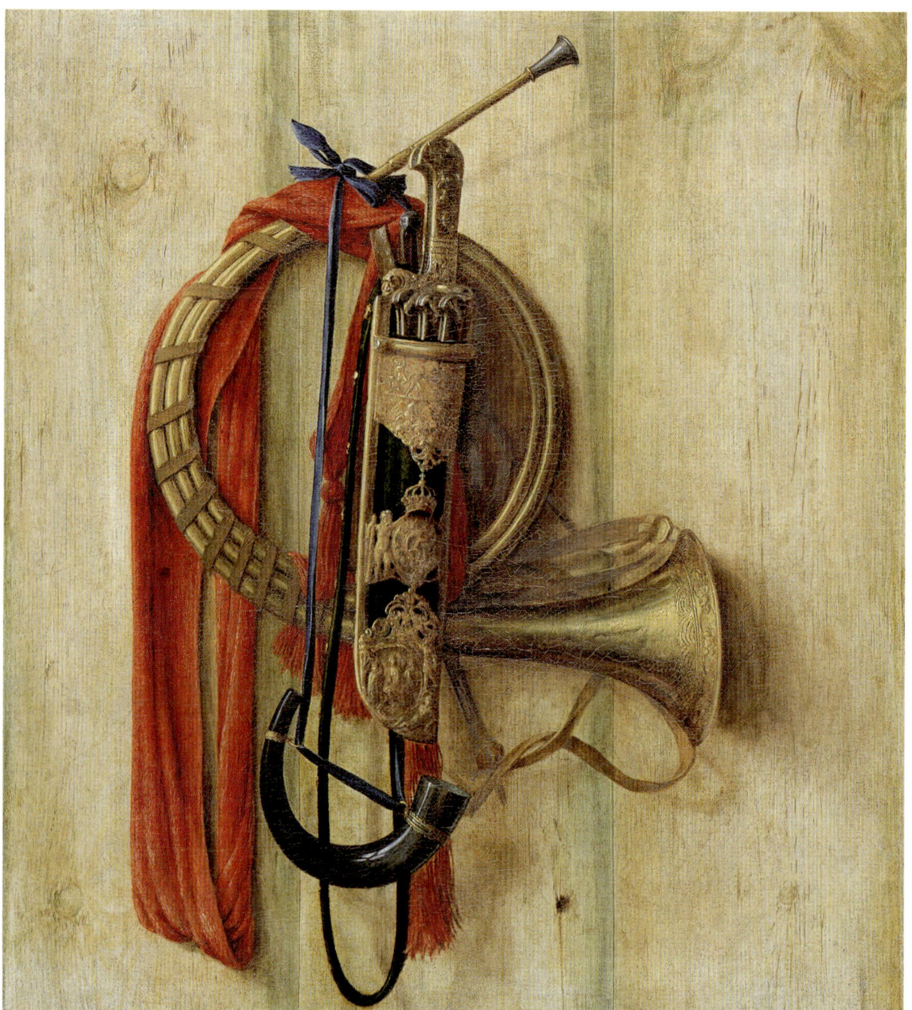

16 Trompe l'Oeil with Hunting Knife and Hunting Horn. Equipment for Riding to Hounds

1671
Oil on canvas, 85.5 x 77.5 cm
Copenhagen, Statens Museum for Kunst

A curled brass hunting horn, a powder horn and the King's hunting knife in a splendid silver gilt-mounted sheath decorated with hunting motifs and the monogram C5 are hanging together with a red sash on a wooden wall consisting of three pale pinewood boards. The light enters from the left. The hunting knife is a Dresden work dating from about 1630; the monogram refers to the eldest son of Christian V, Christian the Prince Elect. The companion to this piece (cat. no. 17) similarly displays royal hunting equipment, which is today preserved in Rosenborg Palace.

17 Trompe l'Oeil with Falconer's Bag and other Equipment for Falconry

Probably about 1671
Oil on canvas, 89.5 x 77.5 cm
Copenhagen, Statens Museum for Kunst

Falconry equipment is displayed in a seemingly haphazard manner, hanging from a tack knocked into a light-coloured board partition. The light in the picture comes from the left, to highlight the pale-coloured hunting bag from which bird's wings stick out in a sharp but soft diagonal, almost as if the bag itself has wings. A falconry hood hangs above the bag; and a falconry lure hangs over it. A similar display of falconry equipment is seen in cat. no. 21.

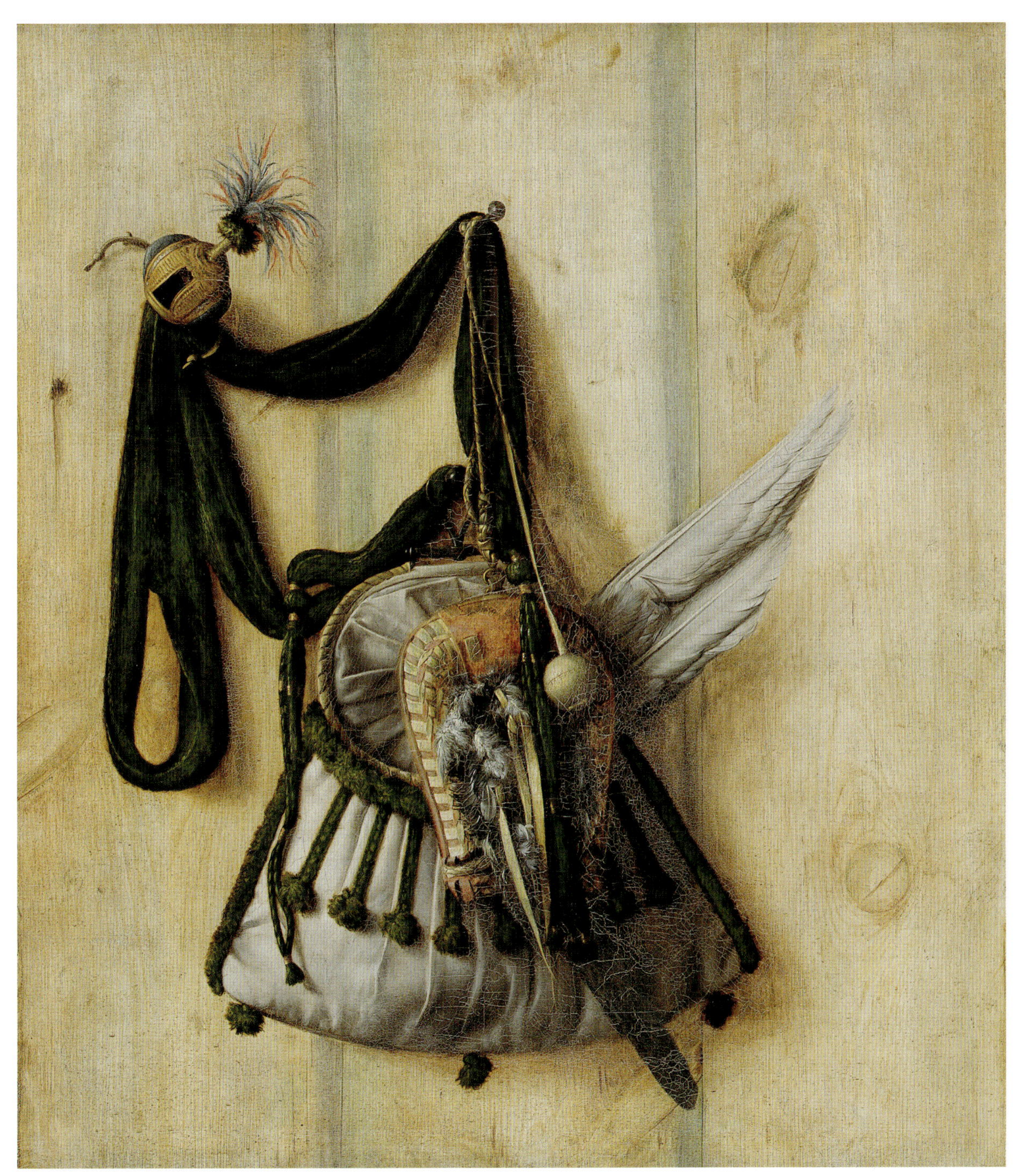

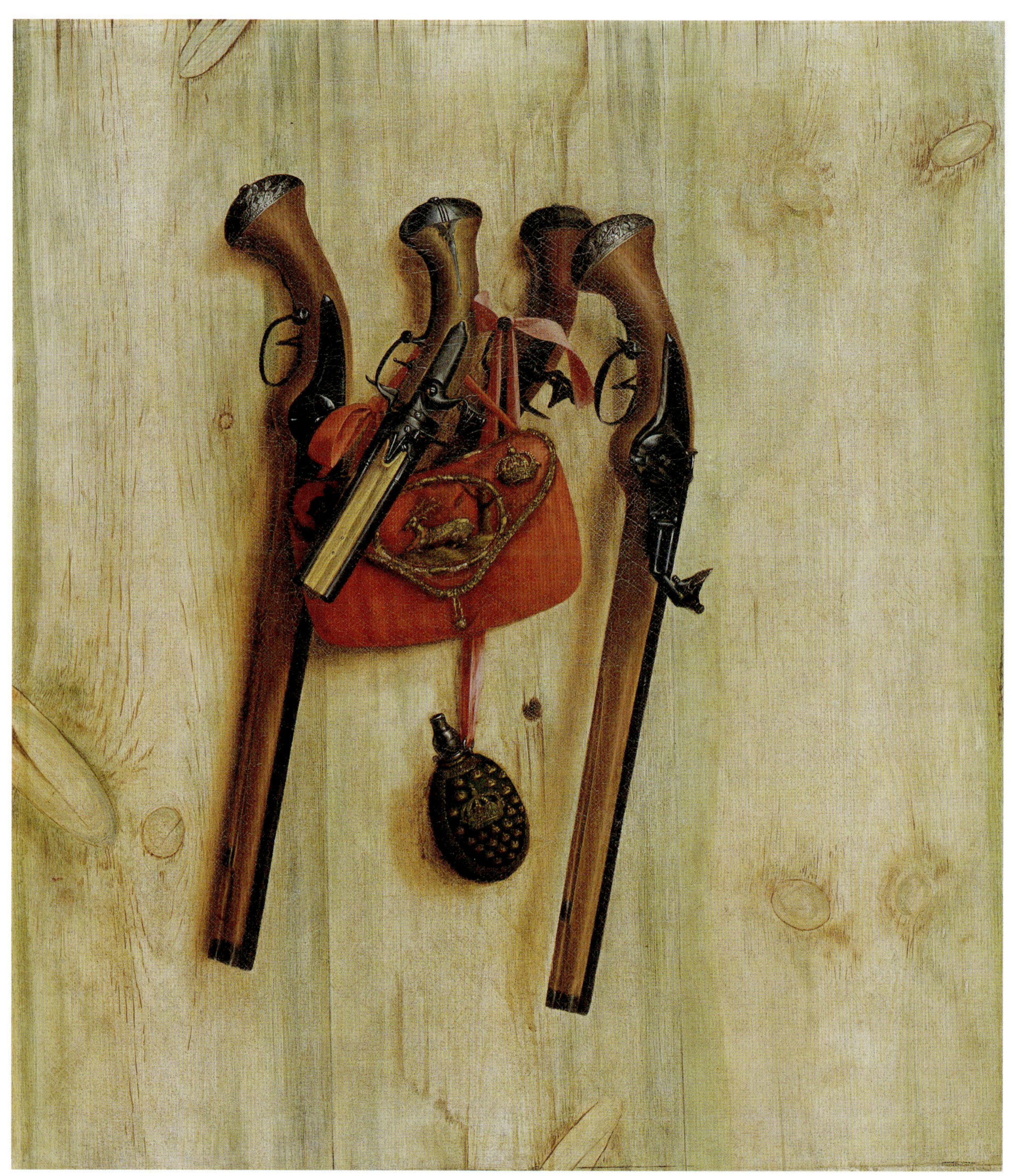

18 Trompe l'Oeil with Pistols

Probably about 1671
Oil on canvas, 89.5 x 77.5 cm
Copenhagen, Statens Museum for Kunst

Four pistols – two long-barrelled and two
pocket pistols – hang uniformly against a
wooden partition together with a bag and
powder container. The bag is embroidered
with a royal crown and a medallion with a
springing stag in a landscape and the powder
container also shows a royal crown. The light
in the picture enters from the right-hand side,
and, in order to reinforce the illusion, the
work would be best placed in a position where
the natural light also entered from the right.

19 Trompe l'Oeil with Riding Whip and Letter Bag

Probably about 1671
Oil on canvas, 90 x 77 cm
Copenhagen, Statens Museum for Kunst

A riding whip, a bag filled with small slips of
paper, a horn(?) and a red and white striped
sash hang on a board in a seemingly random
way. The whip is seen again in cat. no. 21. The
objects all belonged to Christian V, whose
falconry and hunting equipment is depicted in
a number of still-life trompe-l'oeil paintings.

In the third in this series, four pistols and a bag are hanging on a board partition together with a powder container (cat. no. 18), while in the fourth we see among other things a riding whip and a letter bag hanging on two nails knocked into a pinewood wall (cat. no. 19). It has not so far proved possible to identify objects in the third and fourth pictures among the former royal collections.

The two trompe-l'oeil pictures now at Rosenborg are bigger and more representative versions of the first in the above group from the Statens Museum. They contain the same hunting implements as the smaller pictures, but the

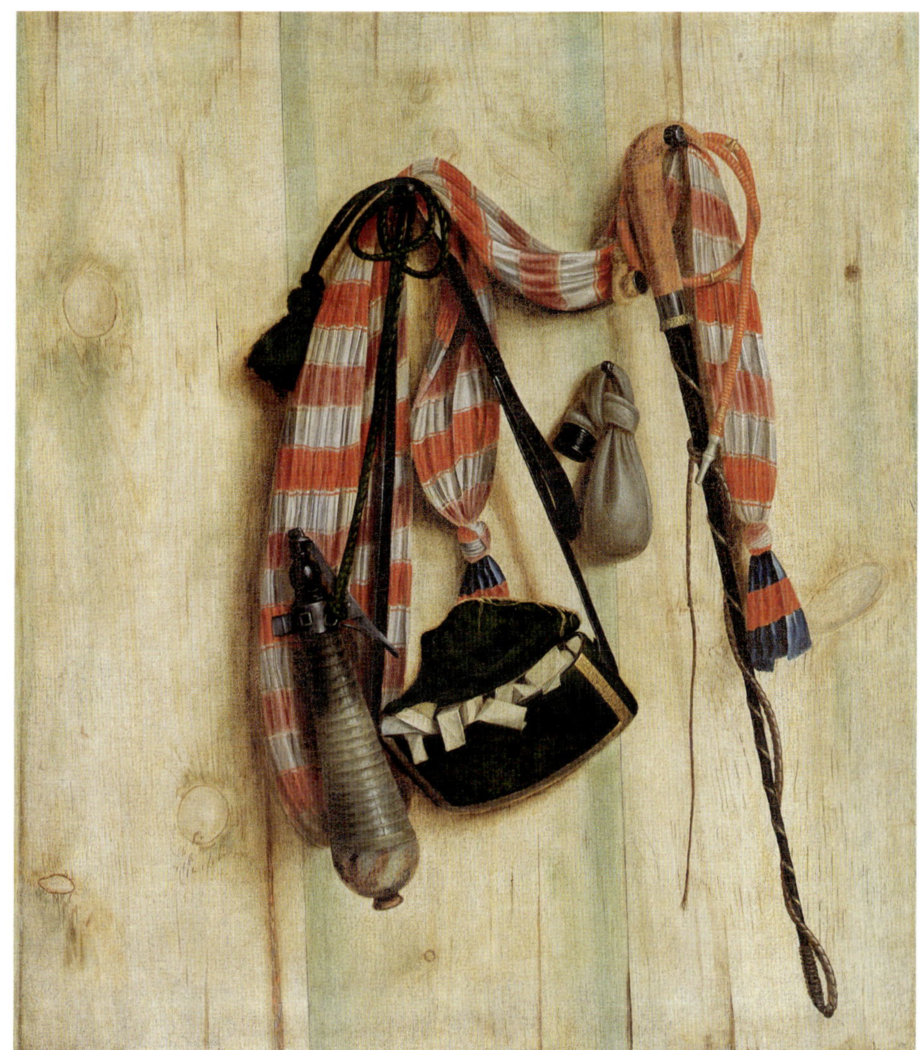

compositions have been expanded in various ways. In the first (cat. no. 20), the equipment for riding to hounds has been supplemented by a hunting sword on the far left and by a blue curtain on the right, drawn aside on a curtain rod which extends across the board partition of the background.

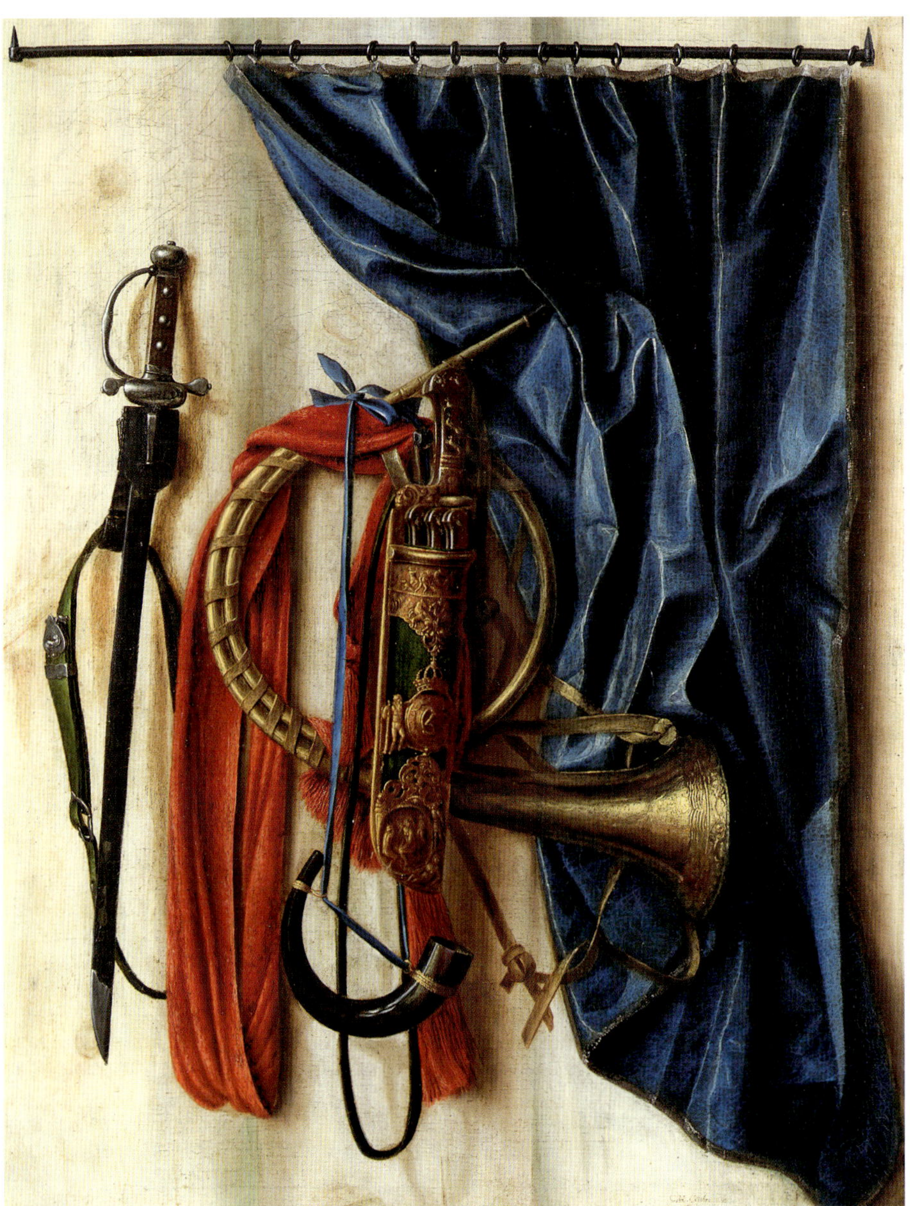

20 Trompe l'Oeil with Hunting Knife, Hunting Horn, Hunting Sword and other Hunting Implements

16[.]2 (probably 1672)
Oil on canvas, 118 x 89 cm
Copenhagen, The Royal Danish Collections at Rosenborg Palace

Here the general theme of cat. no. 16 is embellished with a blue curtain that is pulled back and tucked into a curtain rod that is fixed to the pinewood boards. The attributes of a keen hunter are nonchalantly hung up to present a still life of the King's hunting equipment. Both this and cat. no. 21 were undoubtedly painted for Rosenborg Palace, although both have light entering the picture from the left and curtains pulled to the right. It is difficult to surmise, therefore, how these two paintings may have been intended to hang together.

21 Trompe l'Oeil with
Falconry Equipment and Whip
and Hunting Knife

1672
Oil on canvas, 118 x 89 cm
*Copenhagen, The Royal Danish Collections at
Rosenborg Palace*

The general theme of the King's hunting equipment is here expanded to include the curtain, pulled back over the curtain rod, which is fixed to the boards on which the trompe l'oeil is painted. The curtain is a luxurious addition to the overall composition that includes objects seen in
cat. no. **17**, the bag, falconry hood and lure and cat no. **19**, the rather jaunty riding whip.

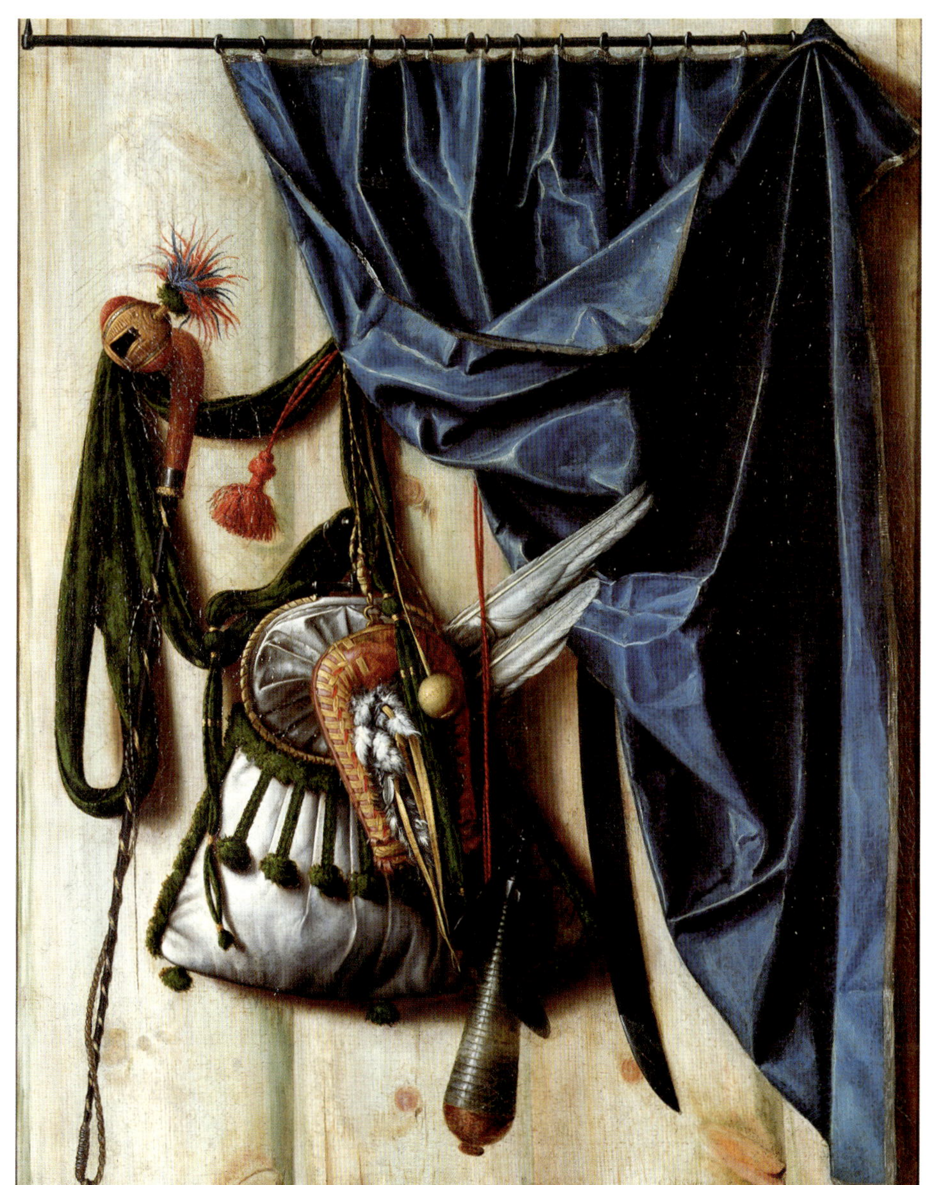

Chantourné Pictures

CHANTOURNÉ (FROM FRENCH, *chantourner*, to cut out with a fretsaw) is a term used for pictures cut out along the outline of an object or human figure, and then painted illusionistically.[43] This type of trompe-l'oeil painting achieved popularity in the seventeenth century, and Arnold Houbraken relates in his *Groote Schouburgh* that the artist Cornelis Bisschop (1630–1674) from Dordrecht was the first to paint cut-out pictures of this kind: 'He was presumably the first, not to say the best, to have the idea and most naturally created different figures "cut out" in wood and painted in a lively fashion with the object of placing them in a corner or a doorway. I have seen some which, in the positions in which they were placed, deceived the eye to such an extent that people greeted them as though they were real persons … But nowadays you only see miserable trash in this field, invented by untalented weaklings, or else pathetic copies of the above-mentioned paintings.'[44] Houbraken also recalls that at the home of his teacher, Samuel van Hoogstraten, he has seen cut-outs of apples, pears and lemons in a bowl, of a slipper or shoe placed in a corner of the room or under a chair, and of salted and dried plaice, painted on canvas and hung up in odd places such as the pantry door, so deceptively executed that people have mistaken them for real plaice.[45]

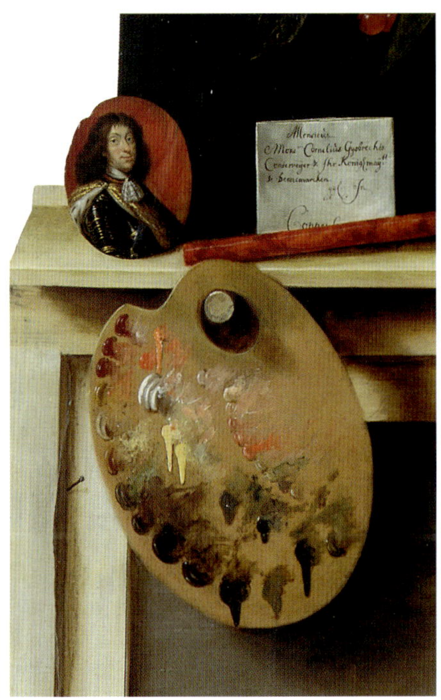

As with the illusionistically painted cupboard door that could open on real iron hinges (cat. no. 14), Gijsbrechts also mixed illusion and reality in his *chantourné* pictures. In 1670 he had the idea of painting a trompe-l'oeil easel on an oak board which had been cut into the correct shape (cat. no. 22). On the easel shelf there is a magnificent still life depicting a gilt goblet and fruit – peaches, cherries, grapes, apples, a melon, a pomegranate, a fig and a peeled lemon are scattered on a marble table partly covered by a dark green table-cloth with golden fringes. The still life is framed by an illusionistic representation of a broad, moulded black frame. In front of the picture are the artist's marbled maulstick and a bunch of brushes. On the right are a paint box divided into three sections, daubed with paint, and a paint rag which, however, is only a fragment, as part of the easel where the top of the maulstick could be seen has broken off and is missing. On the left there is a small oval portrait of Christian V after an original painting by Abraham Wuchters (*c.*1610–1682), a Dutch portraitist working in Denmark. The monarch is dressed in armour and an ermine cloak, and is wearing the Order of the Elephant on a blue ribbon around his neck. Beneath this portrait we see the artist's palette with the paints still wet, and on the floor, leaning against the easel, there is a framed

22 Cut-Out Trompe l'Oeil Easel with Fruit Piece

Probably about 1670
Oil oak, 226 x 123 cm
Copenhagen, Statens Museum for Kunst

The easel, a so-called *chantourné* picture
(from the French to cut with a fretsaw), is
reminiscent of those found in Dutch studio
pictures from the seventeenth century. It has,
together with paintings and painter's tools,
been carved out of a thick oak plank.
The work is intended to be free standing,
supported by a rod that is fixed to the back.
A still life sits on the easel shelf depicting
various fruits, a gilt goblet and
half-full toasting cup in which there is a
half-peeled lemon. The objects are arranged
on a marble table that is partly covered by a
dark green tablecloth with gold fringes.
On the shelf are a number of objects
including a small portrait of King Christian
V, the artist's card and his maulstick. Below
the shelf is a framed picture with its back
turned to the viewer. The small oval portrait
(detail *left*) and the artist's card, stand on the
shelf in front of the still life on the artist's
easel. The portrait is of King Christian V
after a painting by the Dutch portraitist
Abraham Wuchters. The artist's card
distinguishes him as 'Court Painter to His
Majesty the King of Denmark in
Copenhagen.' The maulstick creates a soft
diagonal and would probably have jutted out
from the edge of the still-life painting,
creating a striking *chantourné* effect. The
artist's palette drips with soft wet paints,
seemingly just employed in the still life
propped up on the easel.

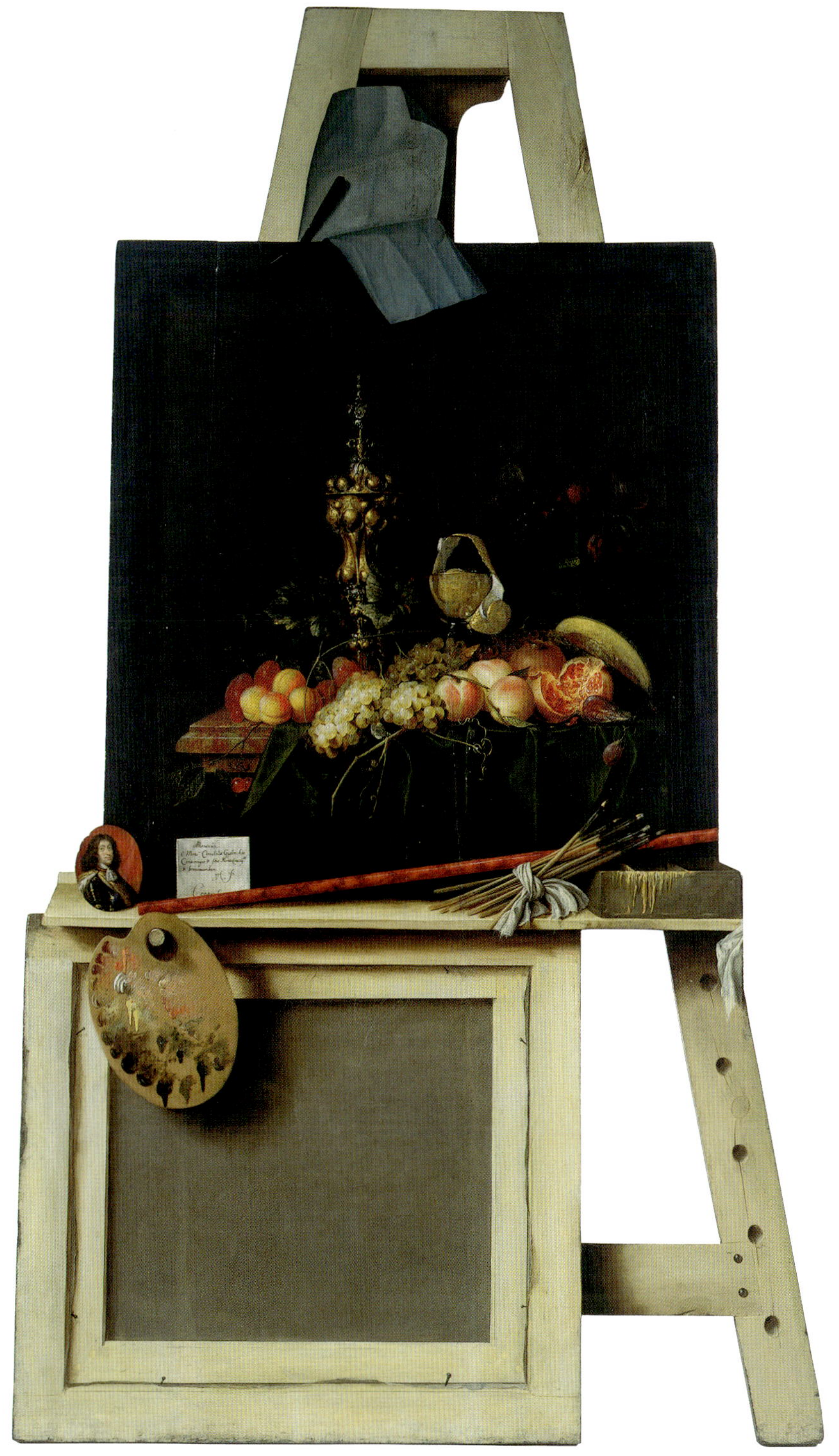

picture with its reverse towards us. Long, thin threads from the ragged edge of the canvas hang down like cobwebs in front of it. Between the maulstick and the still life on the shelf, the artist has inserted a note which, presumably with a certain amount of pride, he has addressed to '*Monsieur/Mons Cornelius Gysbrehts/Conterveijer v. Ihr Königlmay tt/v. Dennemarken/ggl. In/Coppenh*' (Mr Cornelius Gijsbrechts, Court Artist to His Majesty the King of Denmark in Copenhagen). The reputation of this remarkable picture must have spread, for sixteen years later the Italian artist Antonio Forbera (died *c.*1690), who had emigrated to Avignon in France where he was known as Antoine Fort-Bras, made a similar picture, now in the Musée Calvet, Avignon (*fig. 12*),[46] which would be unthinkable without inspiration from Gijsbrechts.

A painting of *The Reverse of a Framed Painting* in Copenhagen (cat. no. 23) can also be viewed as a *chantourné* picture. Both in his large *Easel* (cat. no. 22) and his *Paintings, Painter's Tools and a Flower-Patterned Table-Cover in the Artist's Studio* (cat. no. 7); Gijsbrechts had depicted paintings with their reverse towards us. In his *Easel* it was, as here, a framed painting, but in a dramatic attempt to take this idea to its furthest extreme, he isolated this aspect of the painting and turned it into an independent work of art. The idea is entirely in accordance with the cut-out boards with painted motifs which Houbraken had seen in a corner of Hoogstraten's living room. In just the same way, *The Reverse of a Framed Painting* was not intended to be hung on the wall, but to be placed against it. The viewer would be deceived into trying to turn the picture around, only to see the reverse of an unframed painting. Gijsbrechts had created the paradoxical painting with two backs.

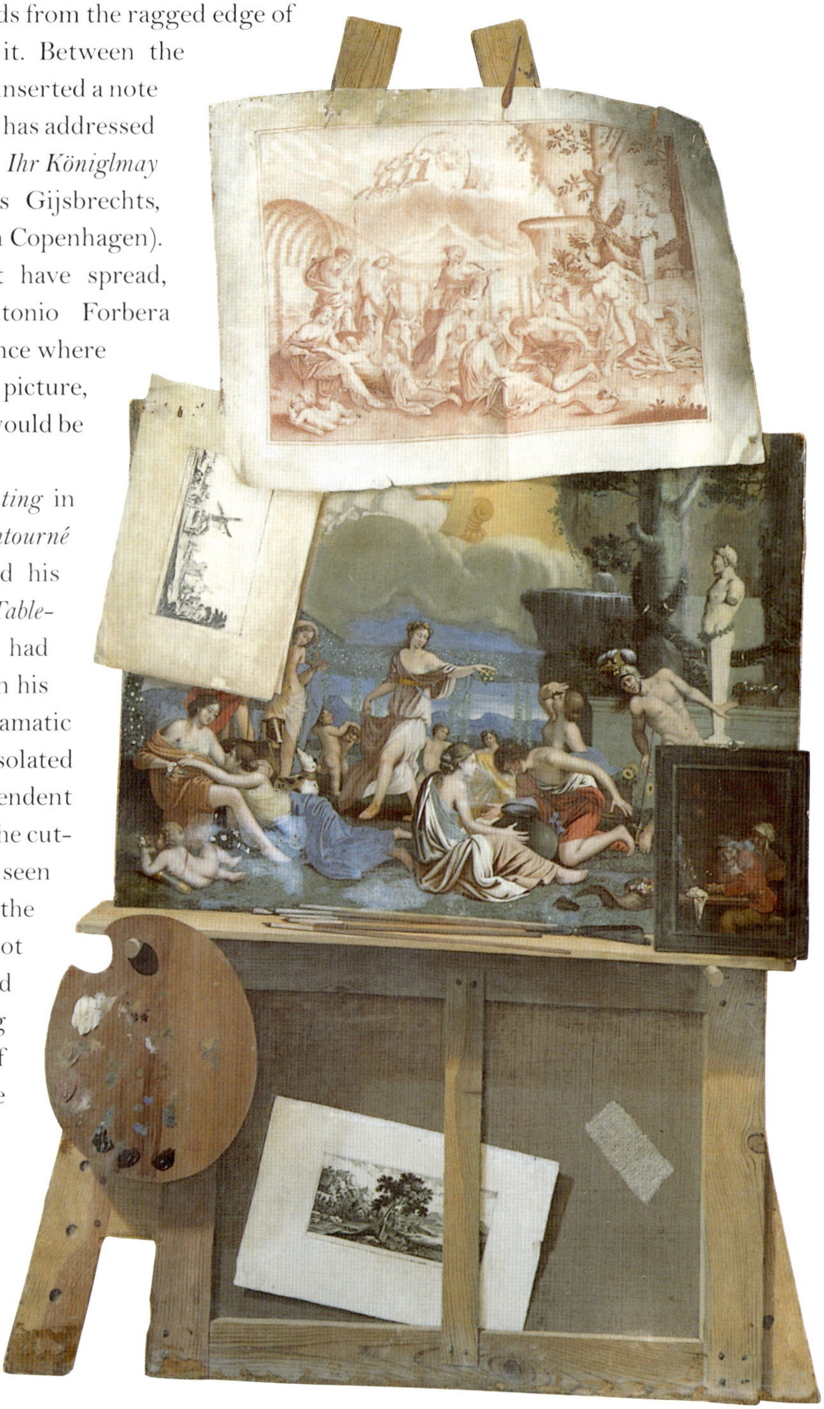

Fig. 12

Antonio Forbera (Antoine Fort-Bras)
Trompe l'Oeil. The Painter's Easel
1686
Oil on canvas, 162 x 95 cm
Avignon, Musée Calvet

23 Trompe l'Oeil. The Reverse of a Framed Painting

1670/72
Oil on canvas, 66.4 x 87 cm
Copenhagen, Statens Museum for Kunst

Gijsbrechts was no doubt aware of the psychological disquiet he would provoke with this trompe l'oeil showing the back of a canvas. The painting is probably intended to be placed against the wall rather than hung, with the intention that the unsuspecting viewer attempts to turn it around – only to see the back of an unframed painting. The painting has 'two backs'. However, the front of this work has a small *cartellino*, or piece of paper, fixed to the canvas with red sealing wax; it bears the number 36. The *cartellino* suggests that the picture is numbered for a collection or art dealer's catalogue but in any case the number removes the picture's anonymity and playfully distinguishes *The Reverse of a Framed Painting* from the back of the trompe l'oeil.

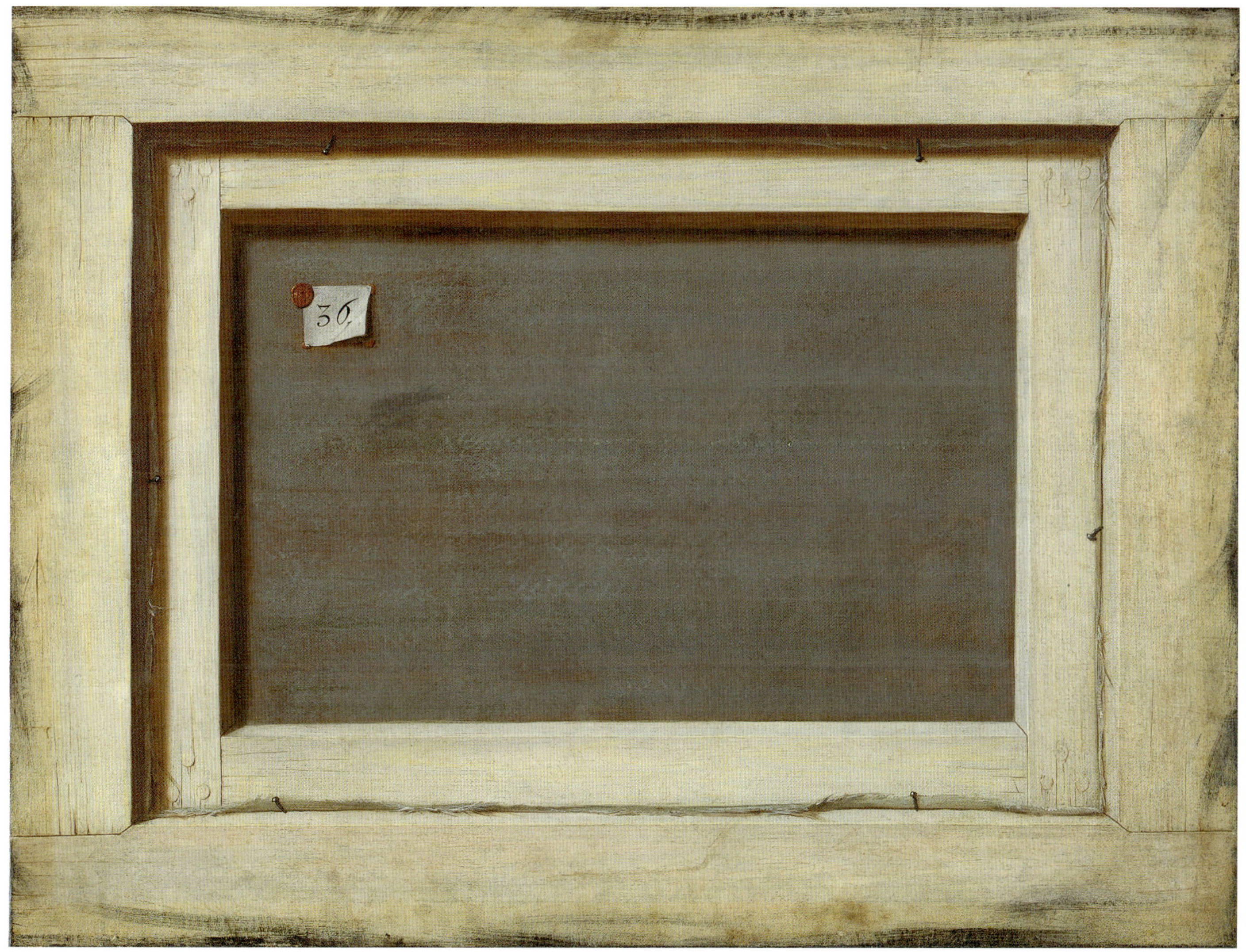

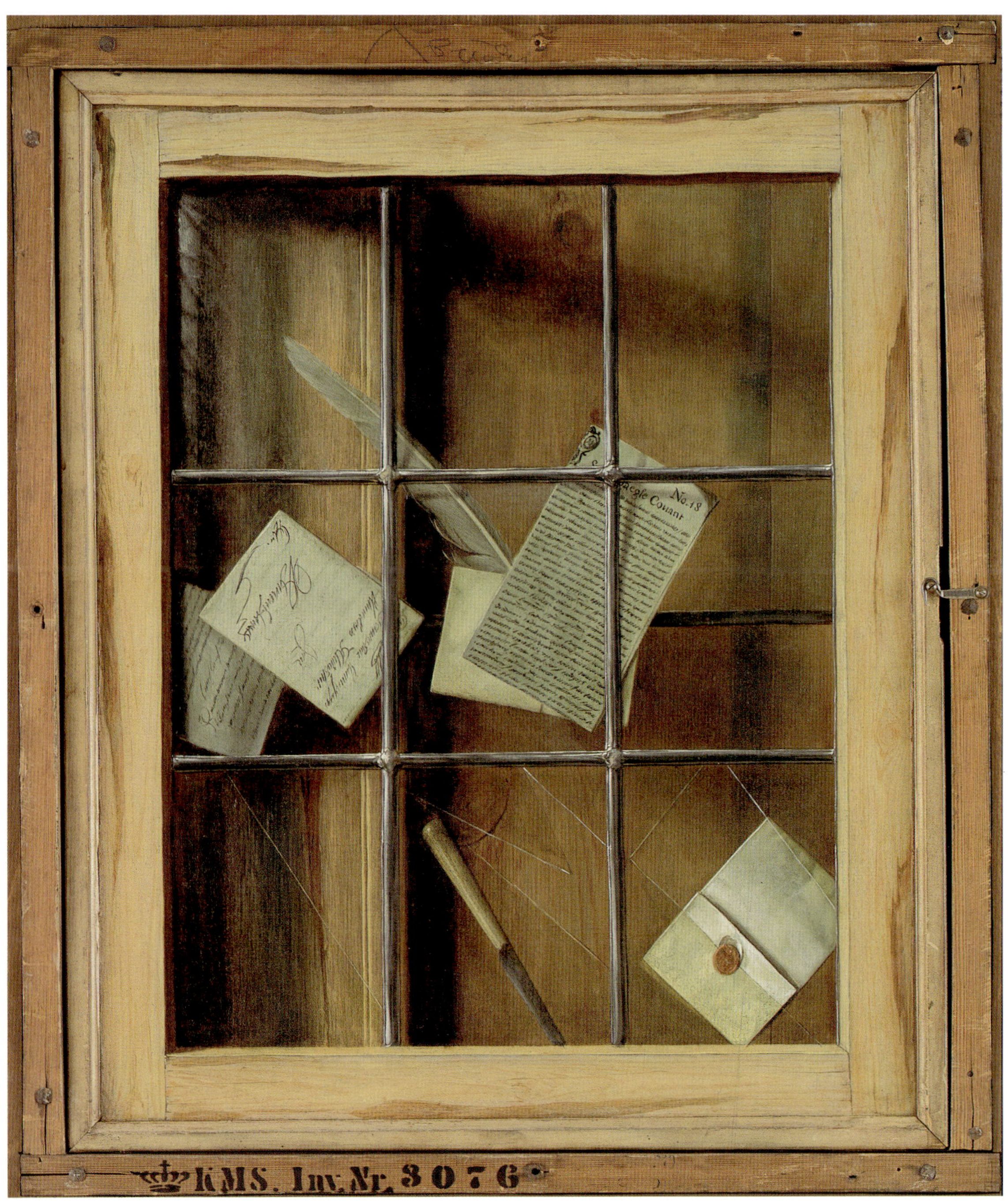

The Legacy of Gijsbrechts

14a Trompe l'Oeil. A Cabinet of
Curiosities with an Ivory Tankard
(reverse of cupboard door)

1670
Oil on canvas, 99.5 x 89.5 cm
Copenhagen, Statens Museum for Kunst

The hinges and the lock on this cabinet are
not an illusion and the door actually opens,
just as the lock can be turned by the key. The
image here shows the 'backs' of objects seen
through the 'front' of the door in cat. no. 14.

DESPITE THE LACK of art-historical evidence relating to Gijsbrechts's life and work, much can be learned from the paintings themselves. It is clear that he was inspired by the art of antiquity, the art of the Renaissance, and by his contemporaries, especially those in the Netherlands. His work contains many references to popular emblematic literature, his two royal patrons and to his absolute commitment to the art of trompe-l'oeil painting, taking the genre beyond its previous limits of 'the decorative pun' to establish an art form rich in innovative ideas, techniques, composition and symbolism.

There can scarcely be any doubt that artistically, technically and intellectually, Gijsbrechts's four years in Copenhagen were a peak in his career as an artist. He developed the whole of his trompe-l'oeil repertoire there, and both the range and quantity of the works executed in Copenhagen are unrivalled in his oeuvre. At no time, before or after, did he so consciously and consistently exploit the artistic potential of still-life and trompe-l'oeil painting. He introduced a new and more monumental version of the motif of the letter rack, as for example with the two vertical letter racks from 1668 (cat. nos. 1 and 2) and the two magnificent letter racks with royal proclamations of 1671 and 1672 respectively (cat. nos. 3 and 4). With his *Studio Wall with Vanitas Still Life* (cat. no. 9), he created a completely new trompe-l'oeil theme which pondered the vocation of the artist and the eternal qualities of art; and in three of his works – the *Cabinet of Curiosities with an Ivory Tankard* (cat. no. 14), in which the glass door can be opened on iron hinges, the *chantourné Easel* (cat. no. 22) and the *Reverse of a Framed Painting* (cat. no. 23) – he went in completely new directions.

His work had a lasting impact on other artists, and his influence can be traced in the astonishing tradition of American illusionistic painting from the nineteenth century right up to the present day.

Notes

1 Siegfried, S.L., 'Boilly and the Frame-up of Trompe l'oeil', *The Oxford Art Journal*, 15, No. 2, 1992, pp. 32–4.

2 It is possible that Jacopo de' Barbari's picture played its part in a specific context and was therefore not an autonomous easel painting.

3 I am deeply indebted to Dr Michael Braun for his generosity in making his unpublished dissertation *Cornelis Gijsbrechts und Franciscus Gijsbrechts* (microfiche), Berlin 1994, available to me.

4 We thus look in vain for his name in Joachim von Sandrart's *Teutsche Academie* (1675–9), Samuel van Hoogstraten's *Inleyding tot de Hooge Schoole der Schilderkonst* (1678) and Arnold Houbraken's *De Groote Schouburgh der Nederlantsche Konstschilders en Schilderessen* (1718–21); see Braun 1994, I, p. 22.

5 See Braun 1994, I, p. 19.

6 Marquard 1918, pp. 56, 58, 68 and 85.

7 Gammelbo 1956, p. 183.

8 Rombouts/van Lerius 1961, p. 302.

9 On the basis of an inscription on the reverse, a small oval *Portrait of an Elderly Woman* (painted on wood) in the Gemäldegalerie der Staatlichen Museen zu Berlin, Preussischer Kulturbesitz (inv. no. B 208) [Gammelbo 1956, p. 138, no. 41; Braun 1994, II, no. 1.1.36] has been thought to represent Cornelius Gijsbrechts's 60-year-old wife in 1672. It has thus been incorporated by Gammelbo and others into the reconstruction of Gijsbrechts's biography, but according to Braun's very convincing interpretation of the inscription, the figure is not Gijsbrechts's wife, but the wife of whoever commissioned the portrait – see Braun 1994, I, p. 21f.

10 See Braun, 1994, I, p. 20.

11 De Monconys 1665–66, vol. II, pp. 372ff, cf; Gammelbo 1956, p. 139f.; Koester et. al. 1999, p. 73 note 30 [Celeste Brusati] and Chong/Kloek, 1999–2000, p. 231.

12 According to Fueszli 1806, p. 503.

13 Hein 1996, p. 31. See also Koester 1999, p. 80 [Jorgen Hein].

14 Hein 1996, p. 31f.

15 Liisberg, Bering, H.C., *Rosenborg og Lysthusene i Kongens Have*, Copenhagen, 1914, p. 140.

16 See Ljungström 1988, p. 31. The picture bought by De la Gardie is not known today. As the payment to the artist is dated 31 March, only three or four days had elapsed before Gijsbrechts received this payment, which, according to Ljungström, is unusually fast for De la Gardie. In Ljungström's view this might suggest that Gijsbrechts was on the point of leaving Sweden.

17 Liisberg 1897, p. 169: '*En frugtstöcke med Contrafeiers instrumenter malet på Perspectiv*' (A fruit painting with a painter's equipment painted in perspective). There is mention of a further three which have previously been overlooked, for the '*Tre Kamfoore malet paa Perspectisk*' (three comb holders [tidies] painted in perspective) can only be *chantourné* tidies by Gijsbrechts, but this does not effect the argument below. The pictures were in the '*Schilderi Gemachet*' (The Painting Chamber).

18 Liisberg 1897, p. 142: '*Tolv kunstige Stykker med adskillige figurer paa af Cornelio Gübsbrecht*' (Twelve artificial pieces with various figures on by Cornelio Gübsbrecht) and '*Et Stykke med Frugter paa og hvad Instrumenter, som hører til en Skilder*' (A piece with fruits and with instruments belonging to a painter). The pictures were in the '*Perspectivsal*' (the Perspective Chamber). There is also a reference to '*Tvende Kamfoere meget vel skildret*' (Two comb holders [tidies] very well depicted), presumably works by Gijsbrechts (see note 17).

19 See Gundestrup 1991–5, II, pp. 420–7. The pictures were in the '*Perspective Kammer bestående af Allehaande Kongelige Perspektiv-Stykker baade udi aaben og inden i Kister skiulte Malerier, saavelsom herlige Stilleben, Frugtstykker og deslige.*' (The Perspective Chamber consisting of all manner of royal perspectives both open and inside chests hidden paintings, as well as splendid still lifes, fruit pieces and the like.) There is also a mention of '*Tvende Kam fouteraler curieux malet*' (Two comb holders [tidies] curiously painted), presumably works by Gijsbrechts (see notes 17 and 18). These two paintings were auctioned in 1824 (see Gundestrup 1991–5, p. 428).

20 In the inventory from 1737 (see Gundestrup 1991–5, II, pp. 420–7), there are references to eighteen paintings plus the *Easel* (cat. no. **22**). Of these, inv. no. KMSst538 *Vanitas Still Life* has since been ascribed to Broder Matthiessen (active 1637–1666), and inv. no. KMS3073, *Trompe* *l'Oeil with Musical Instruments*, is now considered to be a (signed) work by Franciscus Gijsbrechts, while inv. no. KMSst513, a letter rack, has not been seen since 1937. Three of the surviving works are not registered among the eighteen – inv. no. KMSsp811: *Trompe l'Oeil with Breakfast Piece and Goblets* (cat. no. **5**), inv. no. KMSsp812: *Trompe l'Oeil. Paintings, Painter's Tools and a Flower-Patterned Table-Cover in the Artist's Studio* (cat. no. **7**), and inv. no. KMS1989, *The Reverse of a Framed Painting* (cat. no. **23**). So, twenty works have survived plus the *chantourné Easel* out of a total of twenty-one plus the *Easel*. Of these, eighteen plus the easel are thought to be works by Cornelius Gijsbrechts, while one is by Franciscus Gijsbrechts. The two works in Rosenborg (cat. nos. **20** and **21**) and the large *Still Life with the bust of Christian V* at Frederiksborg (which also came from Rosenborg) were never in the Kunstkammer.

21 Marquard 1918, pp. 56, 58, 68, 76, 85. Accounts of this kind are not extant for the period before 1670.

22 See Braun 1994, I, p. 12.

23 See, for instance, examples in the Bayerische Staatsgemäldesammlungen, Munich.

24 Formerly in the Galerie Pardo, Paris. Signed and dated 1657. Reproduced in Ydema, O., *Carpets and their datings in Netherlandish Paintings 1540–1700*, 1991, p. 130, no. 7.

25 See Braun 1994, II, p. 52.

26 For instance, a *vanitas* still life in the Russell collection, Amsterdam (1970), signed and dated 'Cornelius Gijsbrechts. A 1669.' Gammelbo 1956, no 19; Braun 1994, no. 1.1.26. This picture must have been painted during Gijsbrechts's stay in Copenhagen.

27 Braun 1994, II, no. 1.1.7.

28 The picture was at one time on hinges and was therefore presumably used as a cupboard door or an internal shutter for a window.

29 For instance in his *Cupboard Door* in the Akademie der bildenden Künste in Vienna (see Trnek, R., *Die holländische Gemälde des 17. Jahrhunderts in der Gemäldegalerie der Akademie der bildenden Künste in Wien*, Vienna, Cologne and Weimer, 1992, pp. 235ff, cat. 80, reproduced on p. 237).

30 Otto Naumann in his catalogue entry in *Masters of Seventeenth-Century Dutch Genre Painting*, ed. Watkins, J. I., Philadelphia, Berlin and London, 1984, p. 158. See also Kortenhorst-von Bogendorf Rupprath, 1993, p. 276.

31 Becker 1979–80, p. 468.

32 In the two pictures in Ghent (figs. 4 and 5), and the two pictures at Rosenborg, Copenhagen (cat. nos. **20** and **21**), the curtain rod is fixed to the actual board and is thus within the painted frame. In one of the two vertical letter racks in Statens Museum for Kunst, Copenhagen (cat. no. **1**), the curtain rod has been fixed to the board on the left side, but to the illusionistically painted frame on the right side!

33 See Hecht 1989, p. 42f, note 6.

34 The first is dated 1670, the second bears no date, but if they are as closely related as suggested here, the second must have been painted in 1670 (or at the latest 1671).

35 See note 21.

36 Behind the portrait figure there are on the left a pillar and a piece of drapery, and on the right a view of a landscape with a castle. I consider it improbable that it represents the

Danish doctor and anatomist Thomas Bartholin (1616–1680) after a portrait by the German painter Heinrich Dittmers (active in Denmark from 1664 to his death in 1677), as suggested by Braun 1994, II, 1.1.23.

37 Ladis 1982, p. 88, cat. no. 4, illustrated on p. 97.

38 Trnek 1992, pp. 235ff., cat. no. 80, illustrated on p. 237.

39 See Sullivan 1984, pp. 68ff.

40 Hoff, A., Schepelern, H. D. and Boesen, G., *Royal Arms at Rosenborg, I–II*, Copenhagen, 1956, I, no. 18, II, pls. 15:1, 15:2, 16:2–5. The hunting knife (inv. no. 6-139), which is a Dresden work from *c*.1630, originally belonged to Christian, the Prince Elect (1603–47), Christian IV's eldest son. The monogram C5, which could be taken for that of King Christian V, in fact belongs to the Prince Elect. As Crown Prince, Christian, uncle of the later King Christian V, was elected King during the lifetime of his father, Christian IV, he also used the figure 5 in his cipher, cf. Hoff 1977, p. 216, repr. P. 215, colour plate A.

41 Rosenborg, inv. no. 6-118.

42 Rosenborg, inv. nos. 6-133, 6-134 and 6-135 or 6-132 respectively.

43 On *chantourné* pictures, see Wilhelm 1953, pp. 295–304.

44 von Wurzbach, A., *Arnold Houbraken's Grosse Schouburgh der Niederländischen Maler und Malerinnen*, Vienna, 1880, p. 247.

45 Ibid, p. 225.

46 Inv. 22431. Malgouyres/Sénéchal 1998, p. 70, no. XXVIII. See de Loye 1960, pp. 19–24.

Select Bibliography

Battersby, M., *Trompe l'Oeil. The Eye Deceived*, London 1974.

Becker, J., 'Das Buch im Stilleben – Das Stilleben im Buch', *Stilleben in Europa*, Exh. Cat., Münster and Baden-Baden 1979–80, pp. 448–478.

Braun, M., *Cornelis Norbertus Gijsbrechts und Franciscus Gijsbrechts* (microfiche) Ph.d. Dissertation, Freie Universität, Berlin 1994.

Brusati, C., 'Stilled lives: self-portraiture and self-reflection in seventeenth-century Netherlandish still-life painting', *Simiolus*, vol. 20, nr. 2/3, 1990–91, pp. 168–182.

Brusati, C., *Artifice and Illusion. The Art and Writing of Samuel van Hoogstraten*, Chicago and London 1995.

Chong, A., & Kloek, W., *Still-Life Paintings from the Netherlands 1550–1720*, exh. cat., Amsterdam-Cleveland 1999–2000.

Copenhagen Catalogue, *Royal Museum of Fine Arts: Catalogue of Old Foreign Paintings*, Copenhagen 1951.

Dars, C., *Images of Deception – The Art of Trompe-l'Oeil*, Oxford 1979.

Fueszli, *Allgemeines Künstlerlexikon, Zweiter Theil*, Zürich 1806.

Gammelbo, P., 'Cornelius Norbertus Gijsbrechts og Franciskus Gijsbrechts', *Kunstmessets Årsskrift* XXXIX–XLII, Copenhagen 1956, pp. 125–126.

Gammelbo, P., *Dutch Still-Life Painting from the 16th to the 18th Centuries in Danish Collections*, Copenhagen 1960.

Gombrich, E.H., *Art and Illusion. A Study in the Psychology of Pictorial Representation*, Princeton 1960.

Gundestrup B., *Det kongelige danske Kunstkammer 1737*, trans., (The Royal Danish Kunstkammer 1737), I–III, Copenhagen 1991–95.

Hecht, P., *De Hollandse fijnschilders. Van Gerard Dou tot Adriaen van der Werff*, exh. cat., Amsterdam 1989.

Hein, J., 'Ein wiederentdeckter Elfenbeinpokal: Fragen nach möglichen Auftraggebern', *Im Blickfeld. Georg Hinz. Das Kunstkammerregal*, exh. cat., ed. Heinrich, C., Hamburg 1996.

Heinrich, C., (ed.), *Im Blickfeld. Georg Hinz. Das Kunstkammerregal*, exh. Cat., Hamburg 1996.

Hoff, A., 'Royal Danish Hunting Collections', *The Connoisseur*, November 1997, pp. 212–221.

Koester, O., et. al., *Illusions. Gijsbrechts – Royal Master of Deception*, exh. cat., Copenhagen 1999.

Kortenhorst-von Bogendorf Rupprath, C., cat. entries, Judith Leyster: *A Dutch Master and Her World*, exh. cat., Haarlem and Worcester 1993.

Ladis, A., *Taddeo Gaddi. Critical Reappraisal and Catalogue Raisonné*, Columbia 1982.

Liisberg Bering, H.C., *Kunstkammeret – dets Stiftelse og aldste Historie*, Copenhagen 1897.

Ljungström Lars, C., 'Äldre svenska quodlibet-stilleben och meningen med dem', *Konsthistorisk Tidskrift*, LVII, Stockholm 1988, pp. 30–45.

Malgouyres, P., & Sénéchal, P., *Peinture et sculpture d'Italie. Collections du Xve au XIXe siècle du Musée Calvet, Avignon*, exh. cat., Avignon and Paris 1998.

Marquard, E., *Kongelige Kammerregnskaber fra Frederik III's og Cchristian V's Tid*, Copenhagen 1918.

Milman, M., *Trompe-L'oeil Painting. The Illusions of Reality*, Geneva 1982

Monconys, B., *Journal des Voyages de M. de Monconys*, I–III, Lyon 1665–66.

Münster/Baden-Baden, *Stilleben in Europa*, exh. cat., Münster & Baden-Baden 1979–80.

Rombouts & van Lerius (ed.), *De Liggeren en andere historische archieven der Antwerpsche Sint Lucagilde, II, 1629–1729*, (Haag 1864–1876), Amsterdam 1961.

Schepelern, H.D., 'Natural Philosophers and Princely Collectors: Worm, Paludanus and the Gottorp and Copenhagen Collections', *The Origins of Museums,. The Cabinet of Curiosities in Sixteenth- and Seventeenth-Century Europe*, ed. Impey, O., & Macgregor, A., Oxford 1986, pp. 121–127.

Sullivan S. A., *The Dutch Gamepiece*, Woodbridge 1984.

Wilhelm, J., 'Silhouettes and "Trompe-l'oeil" Cut-Outs', *The Art Quarterly*, XVI, no. 4, The Detroit Institute of Arts, Detroit 1953, pp. 295–304.

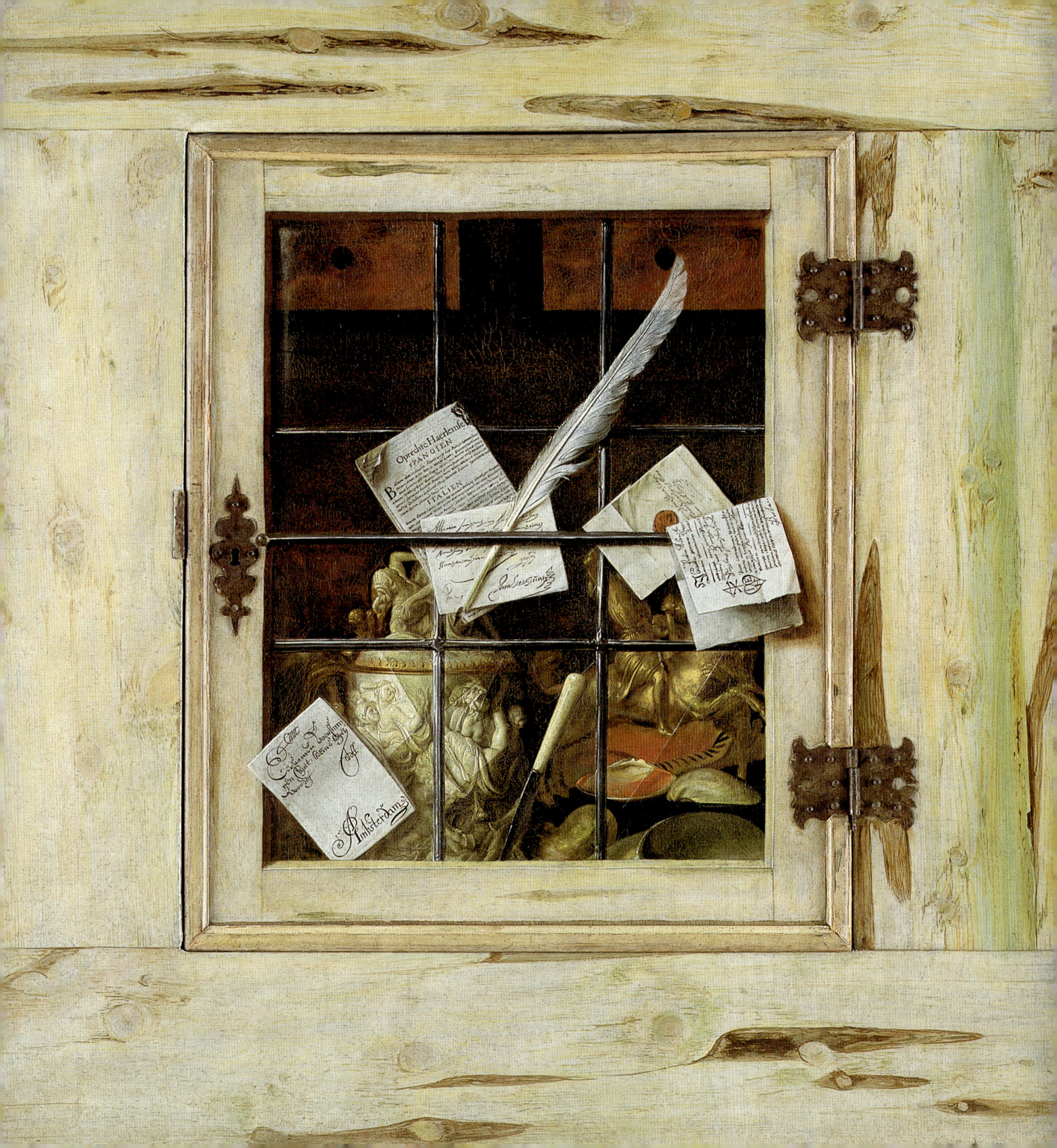

Opredie Haerlemse
SPANGIEN
ITALIEN
Amsterdam

Works in the Exhibition

1

Trompe l'Oeil. Board Partition with Letter Rack and Music Book
1668
Oil on canvas, 123.5 x 107 cm
Signed on landscape print bottom centre: C. N. Gysbrechts. F. A⁰ 1668
Statens Museum for Kunst, Copenhagen, inv. no. KMS3059
Companion piece to cat. no. 2, Statens Museum for Kunst inv. no.
KMS3060

2

Trompe l'Oeil. Letter Rack with a Barber-Surgeon's Instruments
Probably about 1668
Oil on canvas, 125 x 109.5 cm
Statens Museum for Kunst, Copenhagen, inv. no. KMS3060
Companion piece to cat. no. 1, Statens Museum for Kunst inv. no.
KMS3060

3

Trompe l'Oeil of a Letter Rack with Christian V's Proclamation
1671
Oil on canvas, 138.5 x 183 (181.5) cm
Signed bottom right: C. N. Gijsbrechts A⁰ 1671
Statens Museum for Kunst, Copenhagen, inv. no. KMS1902
Companion piece to cat. no. 4, Statens Museum for Kunst, inv. no.
KMS1901

4

Trompe l'Oeil of a Letter Rack with Proclamation by Frederik III
1672
Oil on canvas, 145.5 x 183 cm
Signed bottom left on the empty frame: C. N. Gijsbrechts. A⁰ 1672
Statens Museum for Kunst, Copenhagen, inv. no. KMS1901
Companion piece to cat. no. 3, Statens Museum for Kunst, inv. no.
KMS1902

5

Trompe l'Oeil with Breakfast Piece and Goblets
1672
Oil on canvas, 132 x 183 cm
Signed on base of column on far left: C. N. Gijsbrechts A⁰ 1672
Statens Museum for Kunst, Copenhagen, inv. no. KMSsp811

6

*Trompe l'Oeil with Trumpet, Celestial Globe and Proclamation
by Frederik III*
1670
Oil on canvas, 132 x 201 cm
Signed bottom right on the bench: Cornelius Norbertus Gijsbrechts
F A⁰ 1670
Statens Museum for Kunst, Copenhagen, inv. no. KMSst461
Presumably companion piece or counterpart to cat. no. 7, Statens
Museum for Kunst, inv. no. KMSsp812

7

*Trompe l'Oeil. Paintings, Painter's Tools and a Flower-Patterned Table-
Cover in the Artist's Studio*
Probably about 1670-72
Oil on canvas, 132 x 199 cm
Inscribed on slip of paper on the shelf: *Monsieur/Mons Cornelius
Gijsbrechts/Contervejer v. Ihr. Konigkl/Mayᵗ von Dannemarck/
Coppenhaegen*
Statens Museum for Kunst, Copenhagen, inv. no. KMSsp812
Presumably a companion piece to cat. no. 6, Statens Museum for Kunst
inv. no. KMSst461.

8

Trompe l'Oeil with Violin, Music Book and Recorder
Probably about 1672
Oil on canvas, 117 x 80 cm
Inscribed on a letter bottom right: *A Monsieur/Monsr Gijsbrechts
Kon./terfeyer von Ihr Konigl/ May[t] von DennemarckenL/ggl/In/
Coppenhagen.*
Statens Museum for Kunst, Copenhagen, inv. no. KMS1908

9

Trompe l'Oeil Studio Wall with Vanitas Still Life
1664
Oil on canvas, 87 x 70 cm
Signed on the document: C. N. Gysbrechts 1664
Ferens Art Gallery, Kingston upon Hull City Museums and
Art Galleries, no. 577

10

Trompe l'Oeil with Studio Wall and Vanitas Still Life
1668
Oil on canvas, 152 x 118 cm
Signed bottom right on the vanitas still life: C. N. Gysbrechts. F. A[o]
1668
Inscribed on a slip of paper pushed in behind the stretcher in the bottom
left-hand corner of the vanitas picture: *A Monsuer / Monsuer Cornelius
Norbertus / Gijsbrechts Conterfeÿer ggl. In. / Coppenhagen*
Statens Museum for Kunst, Copenhagen, inv. no. KMSst537

11

Trompe l'Oeil. Still Life of Two Dead Birds Hanging on a Wall
1670/72
Oil on canvas, 77 x 52.2 cm
Statens Museum for Kunst, Copenhagen, inv. no. KMS3030

12

Trompe l'Oeil of a Closed Cupboard.
1665
Oil on canvas, 69 x 59 cm
Signed on the landscape print: C. N. Gijsbrechts A[o] 1665
Musées des Beaux-Arts, Rouen, inv. no. 975.4.75

13

Trompe l'Oeil. An Open Cabinet of Curiosities with a Hercules Group
1670
Oil on canvas, 99.5 x 89.5 cm
Signed bottom right corner (incised): C. N. Gysbrechts A[o] 1670
Statens Museum for Kunst, Copenhagen, inv. no. KMS3075
Companion piece to cat. no. 14, Statens Museum for Kunst, inv. no.
KMS3076.

14

Trompe l'Oeil. A Cabinet of Curiosities with an Ivory Tankard
1670
Oil on canvas, wood and iron, 99.5 x 89.5 cm
Signed bottom right (incised): C. N. Gÿsbrechts A[o] 1670
Statens Museum for Kunst, Copenhagen, inv. no. KMS3076
Companion piece to cat. no. 13, Statens Museum for Kunst inv. no.
KMS3075

15

Trompe l'Oeil with a Dead Duck and Hunting Implements
1670/72
Oil on canvas, 114.3 x 66.8 cm (the picture has undoubtedly been cut on
all four sides)
Statens Museum for Kunst, Copenhagen, inv. no. KMS3012

16

*Trompe l'Oeil with Hunting Knife and Hunting Horn. Equipment for
Riding to Hounds*
1671
Oil on canvas, 85.5 x 77.5 cm
Signed on the powder horn at the bottom: C N Gijsbrechts / 1671
Statens Museum for Kunst, Copenhagen, inv. no. KMS3065
Companion piece to cat. no. 17, Statens Museum for Kunst inv. no.
KMSst460 and forming a series with Statens Museum for Kunst inv. nos.
KMSst460 and KMS3066

17

Trompe l'Oeil with Falconer's Bag and other Equipment for Falconry
Probably about 1671
Oil on canvas, 89.5 x 77.5 cm
Statens Museum for Kunst, Copenhagen, inv. no. KMSst460
Companion piece to cat. no. 16, Statens Museum for Kunst inv. no. 3065
and forming a series with Statens Museum for Kunst inv. nos. KMS3062
and KMS3066.

18

Trompe l'Oeil with Pistols
Probably about 1671
Oil on canvas, 89.5 x 77.5 cm
Statens Museum for Kunst, Copenhagen, inv. no. KMS3062.
Companion piece to cat. no. 19, Statens Museum for Kunst inv. no.
KMS3066 and forming a series with Statens Museum for Kunst
inv. nos. KMS3065 and KMSst460

19

Trompe l'Oeil with Riding Whip and Letter Bag
Probably about 1671
Oil on canvas, 90 x 77 cm
Statens Museum for Kunst, inv. no. KMS3066
Companion piece to cat. no. 18, Statens Museum for Kunst inv. no. 3062
and forming a series with Statens Museum for Kunst inv. nos. KMS3062
and KMSst460.

20

*Trompe l'Oeil with Hunting Knife, Hunting Horn, Hunting Sword and
other Hunting Implements*
16[.]2 (probably 1672)
Oil on canvas, 118 x 89 cm
Signed bottom right (incised): C N Gysbrechts A 16[.]2 (third digit
unreadable). 1672
The Royal Danish Collections at Rosenborg Palace, Copenhagen,
inv. no. 33.27
Companion piece to cat. no. 21, The Royal Danish Collections at
Rosenborg Palace, inv. no. 33.28

21

Trompe l'Oeil with Falconry Equipment and Whip and Hunting Knife
1672
Oil on canvas, 118 x 89 cm
Signed bottom right (incised): C. N. Gysbrechts A 1672
The Royal Danish Collections at Rosenborg Palace, Copenhagen,
inv. no. 33.28
Companion piece to cat. no. 20, The Royal Danish Collections at
Rosenborg Palace, inv. no. 33.27

22

Cut-Out Trompe l'Oeil Easel with Fruit Piece
Probably about 1670
Oil on oak panel, 226 x 123 cm
Inscribed on a card inserted between the maulstick and the 'painting'
on the easel: *Monsieur/Mons Cornelius Gysbrechts/Conterveijer v. Ihr
Königlmay[tt] v. Dennemarcken/ggl. In/Coppenh…*
Statens Museum for Kunst, Copenhagen, inv. no. KMS5 and 995

23

Trompe l'Oeil. The Reverse of a Framed Painting
1670/72
Oil on canvas, 66.4 x 87 cm
Statens Museum for Kunst, Copenhagen, inv. no. KMS1989

Photographic Credits

Bridgeman Art Library, cat. no. 9; John Seyfried 1999, fig. 8;
Scala, figs. 9 and 9a; D. Tragin and C. Lancien, cat. no. 12.

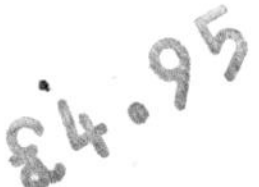